Peugeot
205 T16

Also from Veloce Publishing:

SpeedPro Series
4-Cylinder Engine – How to Blueprint & Build a Short Block for High Performance (Hammill)
Alfa Romeo DOHC High-Performance Manual (Kartalamakis)
Alfa Romeo V6 Engine High-Performance Manual (Kartalamakis)
BMC 998cc A-Series Engine – How to Power Tune (Hammill)
1275cc A-Series High-Performance Manual (Hammill)
Camshafts – How to Choose & Time them for Maximum Power (Hammill)
Cylinder Heads – How to Build, Modify & Power Tune Updated & Revised Edition (Burgess & Gollan)
Distributor-type Ignition Systems – How to Build & Power Tune (Hammill)
Fast Road Car – How to Plan and Build Revised & Updated Colour New Edition (Stapleton)
Ford SOHC 'Pinto' & Sierra Cosworth DOHC Engines – How to Power Tune Updated & Enlarged Edition (Hammill)
Ford V8 – How to Power Tune Small Block Engines (Hammill)
Harley-Davidson Evolution Engines – How to Build & Power Tune (Hammill)
Holley Carburetors – How to Build & Power Tune Revised & Updated Edition (Hammill)
Jaguar XK Engines – How to Power Tune Revised & Updated Colour Edition (Hammill)
MG Midget & Austin-Healey Sprite – How to Power Tune Updated & Revised Edition (Stapleton)
MGB 4-Cylinder Engine – How to Power Tune (Burgess)
MGB V8 Power – How to Give Your, Third Colour Edition (Williams)
MGB, MGC & MGB V8 – How to Improve (Williams)
Mini Engines – How to Power Tune on a Small Budget Colour Ed (Hammill)
Motorsport – Getting Started (Collins)
Nitrous Oxide High-Performance Manual (Langfield)
Rover V8 Engines – How to Power Tune (Hammill)
Sportscar/Kitcar Suspension & Brakes – How to Build & Modify Enlarged & Updated 2nd Edition (Hammill)
SU Carburettor High-Performance Manual (Hammill)
Suzuki 4x4 – How to Modify for Serious Off-Road Action (Richardson)
Tiger Avon Sportscar – How to Build Your Own Updated & Revised 2nd Edition (Dudley)
TR2, 3 & TR4 – How to Improve (Williams)
TR5, 250 & TR6 – How to Improve (Williams)
TR7 & TR8, How to Improve (Williams)
V8 Engine – How to Build a Short Block for High Performance (Hammill)
Volkswagen Beetle Suspension, Brakes & Chassis – How to Modify for High Performance (Hale)
Volkswagen Bus Suspension, Brakes & Chassis – How to Modify for High Performance (Hale)
Weber DCOE, & Dellorto DHLA Carburetors – How to Build & Power Tune 3rd Edition (Hammill)

Those were the days ... Series
Alpine Trials & Rallies 1910-1973 (Pfundner)
Austerity Motoring (Bobbitt)
Brighton National Speed Trials (Gardiner)
British Police Cars (Walker)
Crystal Palace by (Collins)
Dune Buggy Phenomenon (Hale)
Dune Buggy Phenomenon Volume 2 (Hale)
MG's Abingdon factory (Moylan)
Motor Racing at Brands Hatch in the Seventies (Parker)
Motor Racing at Goodwood in the Sixties (Gardiner)
Motor Racing at Oulton Park in the 1960s (McFadyen)
Three Wheelers (Bobbitt)

Enthusiast's Restoration Manual Series
Citroën 2CV, How to Restore (Porter)
Classic Car Bodywork, How to Restore (Thaddeus)
Classic Car Electrics (Thaddeus)
Classic Cars, How to Paint (Thaddeus)
Reliant Regal, How to Restore (Payne)
Triumph TR2/3/3A, How to Restore (Williams)
Triumph TR4/4A, How to Restore (Williams)
Triumph TR5/250 & 6, How to Restore (Williams)
Triumph TR7/8, How to Restore (Williams)
Volkswagen Beetle, How to Restore (Tyler)
Yamaha FS1-E, How to Restore (Watts)

Essential Buyer's Guide Series
Alfa GT (Booker)
Alfa Romeo Spider Giulia (Booker)
BMW GS (Henshaw)
Citroën 2CV (Paxton)
Jaguar E-type 3.8 & 4.2-litre (Crespin)
Jaguar E-type V12 5.3-litre (Crespin)
Jaguar/Daimler XJ6, XJ12 & Sovereign (Crespin)
MGB & MGB GT (Williams)
Mercedes-Benz 280SL-560SL Roadsters (Bass)
Mercedes-Benz 'Pagoda' 230SL, 250SL & 280SL Roadsters & Coupés (Bass)
Morris Minor (Newell)
Porsche 928 (Hemmings)
Rolls-Royce Silver Shadow & Bentley T-Series (Bobbitt)

Triumph Bonneville (Henshaw)
Triumph TR6 (Williams)
VW Beetle (Cservenka & Copping)
VW Bus (Cservenka & Copping)

Auto-Graphics Series
Fiat-based Abarths (Sparrow)
Jaguar MkI & II Saloons (Sparrow)
Lambretta LI series scooters (Sparrow)

Rally Giants Series
Big Healey – 100-Six & 3000 (Robson)
Ford Escort MkI (Robson)
Lancia Stratos (Robson)
Peugeot 205 T16 (Robson)
Subaru Impreza (Robson)

General
1½-litre GP Racing 1961-1965 (Whitelock)
AC Two-litre Saloons & Buckland Sportscars (Archibald)
Alfa Romeo Giulia Coupé GT & GTA (Tipler)
Alfa Tipo 33 (McDonough & Collins)
Anatomy of the works Minis (Moylan)
Armstrong-Siddeley (Smith)
Autodrome (Collins & Ireland)
Automotive A-Z, Lane's Dictionary of Automotive Terms (Lane)
Automotive Mascots (Kay & Springate)
Bahamas Speed Weeks, The (O'Neil)
Bentley Continental, Corniche and Azure (Bennett)
Bentley MkIV, Rolls-Royce Silver Wraith, Dawn & Cloud/Bentley R & S-series (Nutland)
BMC Competitions Department Secrets (Turner, Chambers Browning)
BMW 5-Series (Cranswick)
BMW Z-Cars (Taylor)
British 250cc Racing Motorcycles by Chris Pereira
British Cars, The Complete Catalogue of, 1895-1975 (Culshaw & Horrobin)
BRM – a mechanic's tale (Salmon)
Bugatti Type 40 (Price)
Bugatti 46/50 Updated Edition (Price & Arbey)
Bugatti T44 & T49 (Price & Arbey)
Bugatti 57 2nd Edition (Price)
Caravans, The Illustrated History 1919-1959 (Jenkinson)
Caravans, The Illustrated History from 1960 (Jenkinson)
Chrysler 300 – America's Most Powerful Car 2nd Edition (Ackerson)
Chrysler PT Cruiser (Ackerson)
Citroën DS (Bobbitt)
Cobra – The Real Thing! (Legate)
Cortina – Ford's Bestseller (Robson)
Coventry Climax Racing Engines (Hammill)
Daimler SP250 New Edition (Long)
Datsun Fairlady Roadster to 280ZX – The Z-car Story (Long)
Dino – The V6 Ferrari (Long)
Dodge Dynamite! (Grist)
Drive on the Wild Side, A – 20 extreme driving adventures from around the world (Weaver)
Ducati 750 Bible, The (Falloon)
Dune Buggy, Building a – The Essential Manual (Shakespeare)
Dune Buggy Files (Hale)
Dune Buggy Handbook (Hale)
Edward Turner: the man behind the motorcycles (Clew)
Fiat & Abarth 124 Spider & Coupé (Tipler)
Fiat & Abarth 500 & 600 2nd edition (Bobbitt)
Fiats, Great Small (Ward)
Ford F100/F150 Pick-up 1948-1996 (Ackerson)
Ford F150 1997-2005 (Ackerson)
Ford GT – Then, and Now (Streather)
Ford GT40 (Legate)
Ford in Miniature (Olson)
Ford Model Y (Roberts)
Ford Thunderbird from 1954, The Book of the (Long)
Funky Mopeds (Skelton)
GT – The World's Best GT Cars 1953-73 (Dawson)
Hillclimbing & sprinting – The essential manual (Short)
Honda NSX (Long)
Jaguar, The Rise of (Price)
Jaguar XJ-S (Long)
Jeep CJ (Ackerson)
Jeep Wrangler (Ackerson)
Karmann-Ghia Coupé & Convertible (Bobbitt)
Lambretta Bible, The (Davies)
Lancia 037 (Collins)
Lancia Delta HF Integrale (Blaettel & Wagner)
Land Rover, The Half-Ton Military (Cook)
Laverda Twins & Triples Bible 1968-1986 (Falloon)
Lea-Francis Story, The (Price)
Lexus Story, The (Long)
little book of smart, the (Jackson)
Lola – The Illustrated History (1957-1977) (Starkey)

Lola – All the Sports Racing & Single-Seater Racing Cars 1978-1997 (Starkey)
Lola T70 – The Racing History & Individual Chassis Record 3rd Edition (Starkey)
Lotus 49 (Oliver)
MarketingMobiles, The Wonderful Wacky World of (Hale)
Mazda MX-5/Miata 1.6 Enthusiast's Workshop Manual (Grainger & Shoemark)
Mazda MX-5/Miata 1.8 Enthusiast's Workshop Manual (Grainger & Shoemark)
Mazda MX-5 Miata: the book of the world's favourite sportscar (Long)
Mazda MX-5 Miata Roadster (Long)
MGA (Price Williams)
MGB & MGB GT – Expert Guide (Auto-Doc Series) (Williams)
MGB Electrical Systems (Astley)
Micro Caravans (Jenkinson)
Microcars at large! (Quellin)
Mini Cooper – The Real Thing! (Tipler)
Mitsubishi Lancer Evo, the road car & WRC story (Long)
Monthléry, the story of the Paris autodrome (Boddy)
Morris Minor – 60 years on the road (Newell)
Moto Guzzi Sport & Le Mans Bible (Falloon)
Motor Movies – The Posters! (Veysey)
Motor Racing – Reflections of a Lost Era (Carter)
Motorcycle Road & Racing Chassis Designs (Knoakes)
Motorhomes, The Illustrated History (Jenkinson)
Motorsport in colour, 1950s (Wainwright)
Nissan 300ZX & 350Z – The Z-Car Story (Long)
Pass the Theory and Practical Driving Tests (Gibson & Hoole)
Peking to Paris 2007 (Young)
Plastic Toy Cars of the 1950s & 1960s (Ralston)
Pontiac Firebird (Cranswick)
Porsche Boxster (Long)
Porsche 356 (2nd edition) (Long)
Porsche 911 Carrera – The Last of the Evolution (Corlett)
Porsche 911R, RS & RSR, 4th Edition (Starkey)
Porsche 911 – The Definitive History 1963-1971 (Long)
Porsche 911 – The Definitive History 1971-1977 (Long)
Porsche 911 – The Definitive History 1977-1987 (Long)
Porsche 911 – The Definitive History 1987-1997 (Long)
Porsche 911 – The Definitive History 1997-2004 (Long)
Porsche 911SC 'Super Carrera' – The Essential Companion (Streather)
Porsche 914 & 914-6: The Definitive History Of The Road & Competition Cars (Long)
Porsche 924 (Long)
Porsche 944 (Long)
Porsche 993 'King of Porsche' – The Essential Companion (Streather)
Porsche Racing Cars – 1953 to 1975 (Long)
Porsche Racing Cars – 1976 on (Long)
Porsche – The Rally Story (Meredith)
RAC Rally Action! (Gardiner)
Rallye Sport Fords: the inside story (Moreton)
Redman, Jim – 6 Times World Motorcycle Champion: The Autobiography (Redman)
Rolls-Royce Silver Shadow/Bentley T Series Corniche & Camargue Revised & Enlarged Edition (Bobbitt)
Rolls-Royce Silver Spirit, Silver Spur & Bentley Mulsanne 2nd Edition (Bobbitt)
RX-7 – Mazda's Rotary Engine Sportscar (updated & revised new edition) (Long)
Scooters & Microcars, The A-Z of popular (Dan)
Singer Story: Cars, Commercial Vehicles, Bicycles & Motorcycles (Atkinson)
SM – Citroën's Maserati-engined Supercar (Long & Claverol)
Subaru Impreza: the road car and WRC story (Long)
Taxi! The Story of the 'London' Taxicab (Bobbitt)
Toyota Celica & Supra, The book of Toyota's Sports Coupés (Long)
Toyota MR2 Coupés & Spyders (Long)
Triumph Motorcycles & the Meriden Factory (Hancox)
Triumph Speed Twin & Thunderbird Bible (Woolridge)
Triumph Tiger Cub Bible (Estall)
Triumph Trophy Bible (Woolridge)
Triumph TR6 (Kimberley)
Unraced (Collins)
Velocette Motorcycles – MSS to Thruxton Updated & Revised (Burris)
Virgil Exner – Visioneer: The official biography of Virgil M Exner designer extraordinaire (Grist)
Volkswagen Bus Book, The (Bobbitt)
Volkswagen Bus or Van to Camper, How to Convert (Porter)
Volkswagens of the World (Glen)
VW Beetle Cabriolet (Bobbitt)
VW Beetle – The Car of the 20th Century (Copping)
VW Bus – 40 years of Splitties, Bays & Wedges (Copping)
VW Bus Book, The (Bobbitt)
VW Golf: five generations of fun (Copping & Cservenka)
VW – The air-cooled era (Copping)
VW T5 Camper Conversion Manual (Porter)
VW Campers (Copping)
Works Minis, The Last (Purves & Brenchley)
Works Rally Mechanic (Moylan)

First published in July 2007 by Veloce Publishing Limited, 33 Trinity Street, Dorchester DT1 1TT, England. Fax 01305 268864/e-mail info@veloce.co.uk/web www.veloce.co.uk or www.velocebooks.com.
ISBN: 978-1-845841-29-4/UPC: 6-36847-04129-8
© Graham Robson and Veloce Publishing 2007. All rights reserved. With the exception of quoting brief passages for the purpose of review, no part of this publication may be recorded or transmitted by any means, including photocopying, without the written permission of Veloce Publishing Ltd. Throughout this book logos, model names and designations, etc, have been used for the purposes of identification, illustration and decoration. Such names are the property of the trademark holder as this is not an official publication.
Readers with ideas for automotive books, or books on other transport or related hobby subjects, are invited to write to the editorial director of Veloce Publishing at the above address.
British Library Cataloguing in Publication Data - A catalogue record for this book is available from the British Library. Typesetting, design and page make-up all by Veloce Publishing Ltd on Apple Mac.
Printed in India by Replika Press.

RALLY GIANTS

Peugeot
205 T16

Graham Robson

Contents

Foreword 5
Introduction 7
The car and the team 9
    Inspiration 9
    The Peugeot's importance in rallying 15
    Facing up to rival cars 16
    Timetable – a tight schedule 17
    Homologation – meeting the rules 18
    Engineering features 23
    Peugeot's new M24 project 27
    FF Developments – four-wheel drive specialists 33
    Group B rallying 35
    Second evolution car 37
    The 205 road car 40
    Was the 205 T16 unique? 42
    Building and running the works cars 42
    Intensive use of cars 45
    Personalities and star drivers 54
Competition story 62
    1983 62
    1984 64
    Previous Peugeot rally cars 67
    Peugeot 16-valve engines 72
    1985 80
    Evolution 2 time 92
    1986 97
    Four-wheel drive 104
    2E-The Coventry connection 107
    The 205 T16's successor 116
World Rally success 117
Works Rally cars and when first used 118
Index 123

Foreword

What is a rally? Today's events, for sure, are completely different from those of a hundred or even fifty years ago. What was once a test of reliability is now a test of speed and strength. What was once a long-distance trial is now a series of short-distance races.

In the beginning, rallying was all about using standard cars in long-distance road events, but by the 1950s the events were toughening up. Routes became rougher, target speeds were raised, point-to-point speed tests on special stages were introduced, and high-performance machines were needed to ensure victory.

Starting in the late 1950s, too, teams began developing extra-special versions of standard cars, these were built in small numbers, and were meant only to go rallying or motor racing. These 'homologation specials' now dominate the sport. The first of these, unquestionably, was the Austin-Healey 3000, the first specially-engineered four-wheel drive Group B car was the Peugeot 205 T16, which is profiled here, and the latest is any one of the ten-off World Rally Cars which we see on our TV screens or on the special stages of the world.

Although rally regulations changed persistently over

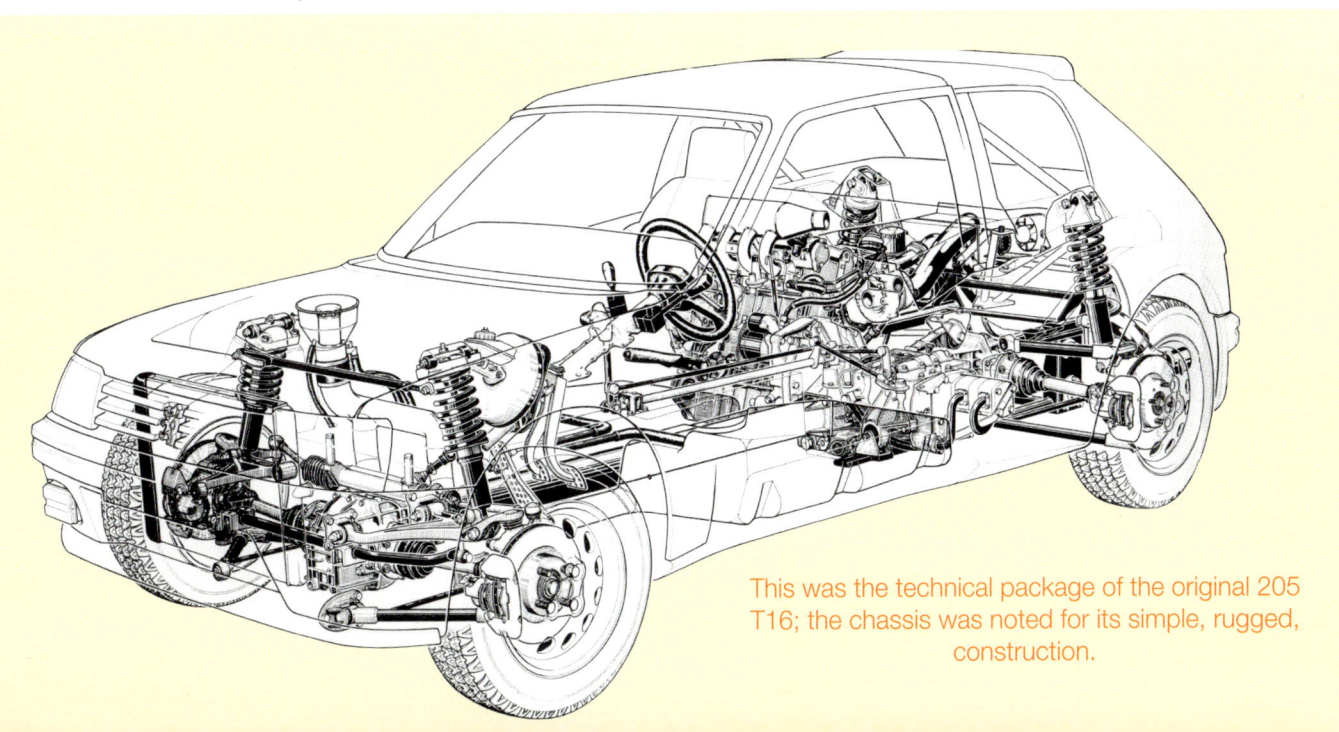

This was the technical package of the original 205 T16; the chassis was noted for its simple, rugged, construction.

the years, the two most important events were four-wheel drive being authorised from 1980, and the 'World Rally Car' formula (which required only 20 identical cars to be produced to gain homologation) being adopted in 1997. At all times, however, successful rally cars have needed to blend high performance with strength and reliability. Unlike Grand Prix cars, they have needed to be built so that major repairs could be carried out at the side of the road, in the dark, sometimes in freezing cold, and sometimes in blazing temperatures.

Over the years, some cars became dominant, only to be eclipsed when new and more advanced rivals appeared. New cars appeared almost every year, but dramatically better machines appeared less often. From time to time rally enthusiasts would be astonished by a new model, and it was on occasions like that when a new rallying landmark was set.

So, which were the most important new cars to appear in the last half century? What is it that made them special at the time? In some cases it was perfectly obvious – Lancia's Stratos was the first-ever purpose-built rally car, the Audi Quattro was the first rally-winning four-wheel drive car, and the Toyota Celica GT4 was the first rally-winning four-wheel drive Group A car to come from Japan.

But what about Ford's original Escort? Or the Fiat 131 Abarth? Or the Lancia Delta Integrale? Or, of course, the Subaru Impreza? All of them had something unique to offer at the time, in comparison with their competitors. Because they offered something different, and raised rallying's standards even further, they were true Rally Giants.

To a rallying petrol-head like me, it would have been easy to choose twenty, thirty or even more rally cars that have made a difference to the sport. However, I have had to be brutal and cull my list to the very minimum. Listed here, in chronological order, are the 'Giant' cars I have picked out, to tell the ongoing story of world-class rallying in the last fifty years:

Car	Period used as a works car
Austin-Healey 3000	1959-1965
Saab 96 and V4	1960-1976
Mini Cooper/Cooper S	1962-1970
Ford Escort MkI	1968-1975
Lancia Stratos	1974-1981
Ford Escort MkII	1975-1981
Fiat 131 Abarth	1976-1981
Audi Quattro and S1	1981-1986
Peugeot 205 T16	1984-1986
Lancia Delta 4x4/Integrale	1987-1993
Toyota Celica GT4	1988-1995
Ford Escort RS Cosworth/WRC	1993-1998
Mitsubishi Lancer Evo	1995-2001
Subaru Impreza Turbo/WRC	1993-2006
Peugeot 206WRC	1999-2003
Ford Focus WRC	1999-2005

There is so much to know, to tell, and to enjoy about each of these cars that I plan to devote a compact book to each one. And to make sure that one can be compared with another, I intend to keep the same format for each volume.

Graham Robson

Introduction & acknowledgements

The Peugeot 205 T16 was not only a phenomenally successful rally car, but as a project it was absolutely ideal for study in all the best business courses. In a very short time, it seems, Peugeot set out a strategy, the T16 did exactly what was planned for it, no big mistakes were made along the way, and its potential was by no means exhausted when it came to an end.

From this opening paragraph, you will see that I am – always have been, in fact – a great admirer of the car, the people behind it, and their strategies. In fact, if I was asked to choose just one car of all those included in the Rally Giants series, as being the most significant, it would probably be Peugeot's 205 T16. Although it wasn't the world's first successful four-wheel drive rally car – that honour goes to the Audi Quattro – it was the elegant Peugeot 205 T16 which made the most impact.

Not only was it an overwhelmingly successful Group B car in the three seasons that this spine-tingling category was at its height, but it combined unique and elegant engineering with real Gallic flair, good looks, and amazing versatility. It was designed for one purpose – to be a supreme works machine – and it delivered on every promise. Like all the best competition cars, its purpose was never blurred (Peugeot never bowed to commercial pressures to make it available to private owners), and at the end of its life it was just as pure as it had ever been.

From start to finish – effectively from 1981 to the end of 1986 – the 205 T16 was designed to make Peugeot supreme in the increasingly colourful world of international rallying, and nothing was allowed to get in the way of that aim. Inspired by that ruthless and determined little man, Jean Todt, generously backed by the Peugeot board, and matured after gathering an enormous amount of rallying expertise into one organisation, the Peugeot team hit the ground running in 1983, and never failed in any of its objectives.

This, then, is the story of one company's determination to reach the pinnacle of Group B rallying, to do it successfully, and never to settle for second best. Right from the start, Peugeot set out to make the world's best four-wheel drive rally car, and let nothing except the limits of the regulations get in its way. The fact that 200 road cars had to be built to secure homologation was taken into account from the beginning – and Peugeot satisfied not only the letter, but the spirit, of the regulations in doing just that!

For rally enthusiasts and engineers alike, the way in which this was done was a credit to everyone concerned. Except for the marketing need to make the new rally car look somewhat like the new 205 road car, every aspect of the 205 T16 was carefully analysed, optimised, and refined. As far as can be seen, there were no serious compromises – for the structure, engine, four-wheel drive transmission, and ease of servicing were all just as good as the state of the art would allow.

Not only did Jean Todt insist on setting Peugeot's best brains to designing 'his' new rally car, but he also extracted a big enough budget from management so that he could hire the world's most charismatic driver – Ari Vatanen – and one of France's most respected testers – Jean-Pierre Nicolas, to complete the jig-saw.

It was to Todt's eternal credit that he signed Timo Salonen to complement Vatanen's skills in 1985, that he lifted the team's shattered morale after Ari's dreadful accident in mid-1985, and that he made the inspired choice of signing up the young Juha Kankkunen for 1986.

Not only that, but along the way Todt's team secured the World Makes Championship in both of the years that the T16 contested a full programme – 1985 and 1986 – and that Peugeot drivers also won the World Drivers' Championship in those years, too – Salonen in 1985 and Kankkunen in 1986. Even after the T16 was banned from World rallying by a change of regulations, evolutions of the same magnificent design were still capable of winning in 'Raid' rallies in the African deserts, up the Pikes' Peak Hillclimb in Colorado, USA, in rally-cross, ice racing, and any other type of motorsport for which it was eligible. Not only that, in due course the 205 T16 Grand Raid would morph into the 405 T16 Grand Raid, and eventually there would be a Citroën ZX Rallye Raid car which also owed much to Todt's original inspiration.

It is a measure of the importance of this car that almost everything and everyone connected with it went on to greater things. I have already noted how the car itself spawned other iterations, and new models which were also successful. Jean Todt not only oversaw the development of Peugeot's Le Mans-winning 905s, but eventually moved to Ferrari in the 1990s, set up 'Team Schumacher', and eventually became Ferrari's CEO. Ari Vatanen returned to robust health, and carried on winning events and hearts all around the world, while Juha Kankkunen moved from team to team as a world-class driver who was competitive until the very end of the century.

In every way, for sure, the 205 T16 was a Rally Giant.

Acknowledgements

In assembling all the facts, figures and illustrations for this book, I want to thank two kind individuals for making my job even more pleasurable.

Every year, Martin Holmes Rallying produces a magnificent survey of the season's rallies, not only at world, but at many other levels too. The first such annual - *World Rallying 1* - covered the 1978 season, and at the time of writing a continuous run of 29 such volumes has made a study of rallying, rally cars, and individuals both absorbing and enjoyable.

Many of the facts and statistics which appear in these pages have been verified and double-checked against *World Rallying*, making a difficult job that much easier.

In addition, I want to give a big 'Thank You' to Gail O'Dell, Des O'Dell's gallant widow, who made assembling the illustrations for this colourful book so much easier. Not only did she let me see Des' invaluable collection of 205 Turbo 16 images (which Peugeot Talbot Sport had provided over the years), but she very graciously allowed me to reproduce many of them in these pages.

I hope – no, I am sure – that their kindnesses have helped to make this book authoritative.

Graham Robson

The car and the team

Inspiration

It was a combination of the success of Audi's new four-wheel drive turbo Quattro, and of the World rally success quite unexpectedly gained by the company's British-based Talbot Sunbeam-Lotus team in 1981, which persuaded Peugeot to build a new and special rally car of its own – the Peugeot 205 Turbo 16 (or 'T16' for short). Corporate and national pride, too, came into the reckoning, and there is no doubt that Peugeot was always serious about its intentions for this project, from the very day that the car was conceived in 1981.

This was a period in which world rallying was rapidly becoming a high-profile, publicity-worthy business to be in, and it was one in which a successful contender demonstrably helped the sales of the less exotic road cars. Not only that, but the reputation of mundane machines could then be glamorised, especially if the marque had been able to win high-profile events such as the Monte Carlo and Safari rallies.

Ford's fortunes in rallying offered a perfect example. Even though almost every Ford Escort of the 1960s and 1970s was a cheaply-specified, mechanically-simple saloon, intended for use by family men, business owners, and hire fleets, the exploits of heroes like Roger Clark, Ari Vatanen and Hannu Mikkola in special (and expensive) rally versions made them extremely fashionable. Later, Lancia's stumbling, rust-prone image for its very ordinary road cars had been transformed in Europe by the success of the glamorous Ferrari-engined Stratos, while at this time even Fiat, Italy's mass-market provider, was benefiting from the image boost delivered by rally successes with the exotic and rare 131 Abarth saloon.

In the 1960s, Peugeot rally successes were gained in rough, long-distance, rallies with saloons like the 404, as driven here by Nick Nowicki to win the East African Safari of 1968.

Driving nothing more powerful than an 80bhp Peugeot 404 model, Bert Shankland won the East African Safari Rally in 1967.

Up until the 1960s, Peugeot had largely ignored motorsport, even though its customers discovered how solid the larger cars could be on the roughest of events, though in the 1970s it relented so far as to set up a modest little works operation at Sochaux, in eastern France, to prepare a series of conventionally-engineered 504-based models (front-engine/rear-drive machines, latterly with powerful V6 engines) for highly paid drivers (not French, to Peugeot enthusiasts' intense irritation) to win in rough and tough events as far flung as the East African Safari, and Bandama in West Africa.

When motorsport's Paris-based authority (the Federation Internationale d'Automobile – the FIA) decided to re-jig the eligibility regulations covering rallying, Peugeot

Christine Dacremont chose the all-independent suspension 504 to tackle the UDT World Cup rally of 1974.

Sheer driving bravery sometimes made up for a lack of performance! In the 1975 rally of Morocco, Hannu Mikkola/Jean Todt won outright in an underpowered 504 saloon, with this sister car (driven by Bernard Consten) in second place.

Mission accomplished, phase 1: (left to right) Guy Frequelin, Henri Toivonen, Paul White, Des O'Dell and Jean Todt toast the Sunbeam-Lotus victory in the 1980 RAC Rally. A year later Todt would be the team boss of a new Paris-based organisation, and the 205 T16 project would be under way.

Left: By 1981, the Peugeot-Talbot works team was competitive at World Rally Championship level, and was based in historic premises in Coventry. With a very small fleet of Sunbeam-Lotus cars, it won the 1981 World Championship for Makes.

Below: Chrysler's (later Peugeot-Talbot's) Sunbeam-Lotus was the true ancestor of the 205 T16, though it had a conventional front engine/rear-drive layout.

Above: "To win the World Championship", team manager Des O'Dell quipped, "everyone told me I needed a better Escort. So I built one ..." In 1980 and 1981, Jean Todt was Guy Frequelin's co-driver in Sunbeam-Lotus cars like this.

Simple, rugged, British rally car engineering – not what Jean Todt wanted from his Group B car, but the rallying heritage and expertise offered by the Talbot Sunbeam-Lotus was exactly what was needed.

Below: In the days before four-wheel drive changed the rally scene, Peugeot-Talbot dabbled with producing a mid-engined/rear-wheel drive version of the front-drive Chrysler Horizon with which to go rallying. Lotus built this one-off prototype for it – neat, and it might have been effective – but the Audi Quattro then changed everything.

listened carefully, studied what was proposed, and when that upheaval was seen to include a new Group B category (where not only four-wheel drive would be allowed, but where only 200 identical cars would have to be produced for a new model to qualify), the company sat up and took notice.

By this time Peugeot, of course, had almost stumbled upon World rallying success by chance. Having bought up Chrysler-Europe in 1978, an ailing business which not only included Simca of France, but the ex-Rootes group operation known as Chrysler-UK, it discovered that Chrysler-UK

14

already had a very competent and cost-effective motorsport operation with an illustrious record. Not only had that little operation recently produced a series of competent racing saloons, but in 1968 its Hillman Hunter had won the very first intercontinental rally, the London-Sydney Marathon.

Even before the takeover was concluded, a prototype of what would become the Chrysler Sunbeam-Lotus had been built in Coventry, and the marketing decision had already been taken that this Lotus-engined hatchback (front-engine/rear-drive – a car which team manager Des O'Dell always described as "a better Escort") should go into production in 1979.

In the end it was Lotus who would carry out the final assembly of this model in Norfolk (it was renamed Talbot Sunbeam-Lotus from mid-1979), the first praiseworthy rally outings came in 1979, and the first World victory followed in 1980. In the following year, a combination of rock-solid preparation, brave driving, lots of rally-craft and some sheer good fortune brought the World Manufacturers' Championship to Coventry.

This, therefore, was the inspiration behind the birth of the 205 T16 – a new Group B, a blooming reputation in rallying, and a desire from Peugeot to transform its marketing strategy. At that time, the general public did not know that a new generation hatchback range, the 205, was planned, this being a much more elegant machine than anything which had previously come from Peugeot, and a successful new rally car to be based on that model would obviously provide a real image boost. And so it was – well before Peugeot's new subsidiary brand, Talbot, had won the World Manufacturers' Championship of 1981, Peugeot's Chairman Jean Boillot had agreed a new strategy. Every step was planned in advance, to the great credit of Peugeot no aspect of it was cancelled, and a newly-appointed motorsport boss, Jean Todt, was directed to make it happen.

At a press conference held in London soon after the end of the 1981 rally season (immediately after Talbot had won the World Rally Championship), Todt outlined a new strategy, making it very clear that he had the backing of Peugeot, from board level downwards. At this conference he made several promises:

Peugeot was to design a new and specialised Group B rally car, which would have four-wheel drive (even though it was newly-crowned as Champion, the Talbot Sunbeam-Lotus was rear-drive only, and therefore vieux jeu).

The new car would be unveiled early in 1983.

Homologation and the first works entries would follow in 1984.

Todt insisted that by 1985 the car would be good enough, as would the team, to win the World Championships.

The name 'Audi Quattro' was not seriously mentioned at this presentation, but effectively this was the 'elephant in the room', for it was the four-wheel drive Quattro which had suddenly transformed the way in which serious competitors would have to tackle rallies in the future.

Although Todt was, and still is, an outwardly opinionated man whom it is quite easy to dislike, he is also a man of great integrity, with an impressive CV. At the time there were many experienced rallying observers ready to write off those brave words as just that – brave words – but four years later they had to make fulsome apologies, for each and every prediction had been fulfilled.

The Peugeot's importance in rallying

Like the Lancia Stratos that had preceded it, in another era (but only a few years earlier), the new Peugeot signalled a complete step-change in the increasingly high-tech sport of world rallying. As with the Stratos, the new Peugeot was conceived by a visionary family-controlled management which could identify the challenge, and realised that it would take much investment to meet that challenge, but was nevertheless determined to do the job properly.

The new Peugeot, in fact, was the world's very first purpose-built four-wheel drive rally car – designed and developed to meet, satisfy, and subtly circumvent the new Group N regulations – Peugeot wanted it to win rallies, and even to win World Championships, and no compromise would be allowed to interfere with those aims. Not only that, but it was always going to demonstrate how a four-wheel drive rally car ought to be conceived and engineered – and not merely cobbled together using existing parts from another model.

Although the world's first competitive four-wheel drive rally car had been the Audi Quattro of 1980, that car was always seen (even by Audi, when it occasionally admitted it) as a clever conversion of a newly-engineered front-wheel drive car, rather than as a completely new approach to the problem. Without the still-secret 90-based Quattro Coupé, and without the four-wheel drive installation of the VW Iltis military vehicle which already existed, the turbocharged Quattro could not have been brought to market at the time when it appeared.

With the new Peugeot, however, it was all going to be very different. Although the thinking was that the basic style would look like that of a new Peugeot hatchback (the 205) which was already being engineered, almost every component, and all the engineering which was hidden away, would be especially developed. On the assumption that it would deliver on all the hopes and dreams – and, knowing Peugeot's record, why should it not do that? – it would set new standards which all other rally teams would have to match in the years to come.

Facing up to rival cars

When Peugeot decided to design a new Group B rally car it was almost, but not quite, a pioneer. Although Audi had started using the turbocharged Quattro Coupé in 1981, this was originally developed as a Group 4 car to meet earlier regulations, for which four-wheel drive had only been authorised since 1979. Since Group B (which required 200 identical cars to be built, with a further 20 'Evolution' models allowed if a manufacturer could develop those at the same time) was not due to come into force until 1 January 1982, Peugeot was to be a real pioneer.

By the time that the new 205 T16 was homologated (1 April 1984), the opposition had already begun to build up, and by the time the Peugeot was at the peak of its powers in 1986, almost every other serious rally team had a rival four-wheel drive car as well. These, then, were the Group B rivals which the Peugeot eventually had to face:

Audi Quattro (long-wheelbase – A1 and A2) – front-engine/four-wheel drive. First used in 1981 (A1: Group 4), and re-homologated (A2: Group B) in May 1983. With turbocharging, the five-cylinder engine produced more than 320bhp, which was originally a step change higher than all its earlier rivals. With a far-forward engine position and weight distribution, and a structure which was too heavy, this was always a compromised layout, but was originally very successful because it was the only such four-wheel drive car in rallying at the time.

After re-homologation in 1983, the 'A2' was lighter and, with 340bhp, a world leader for a short time. Although the T16 had to face it in 1984, it was soon to be replaced at Audi by …

Audi Quattro Sport S1 (short-wheelbase) – front engine/four-wheel drive. Derived from the earlier Quattro A2. Launched at the end of 1983, but first rallied in mid-1984 (after the T16 had made its debut), this had a 12.6in shorter wheelbase, and was several hundred pounds lighter than the A2 Quattro, with a 20-valve engine producing up to 440bhp in rally trim. Very fast in a straight line, but with even more weight up front, it never handled well, and the drivers disliked it. The second evolution type (E2), homologated in mid-1985, addressed these problems by moving many heavy items into the boot to improve the weight distribution, and it had many aerodynamic aids, including a massive rear spoiler. According to independent engineers this car was developed beyond its natural limits, and was not a consistent success.

Citroën BX 4TC – front engine/four-wheel drive. Citroën (a company which was already owned by Peugeot, but which was allowed to operate separately in many ways) should have been ashamed of this lash-up and, in later years, apparently it was. Developed at minimal cost, the 4TC had a far-forward engine, a too-heavy five-door shell, and a simple four-wheel drive transmission which even lacked a centre differential. With 380bhp from 2.1-litres, it was only adequately fast, suffered from heavy understeer, and started only three World rallies in 1986 before the whole project was abruptly cancelled. I don't think a 4TC ever won an event.

Ford RS200 – mid engine/four-wheel drive. Though too heavy in standard form, this designed-for-a-purpose rally car was elegant (the GRP/Kevlar style was by Ghia) and effective. According to the drivers, it handled better than any other Group B machine, and had a better ride on rough surfaces. Started late, as a project (after the unsuccessful rear-drive Escort RS1700T was cancelled), it only ran in World rallies in 1986, before Group B was cancelled. Initially with a 450bhp/1.8-litre engine, the works rally cars needed more grunt – which was planned (2.1-litres/550bhp) for 1987 – but Group B's cancellation killed it off. Peugeot and Lancia both feared this car's potential. At European level it won 19 events in its single season, before becoming a dominant rallycross machine.

Lancia Rally 037 – mid engine/rear-wheel drive. Lancia paid the penalty for being too early with the 037. Announced in late 1981, this pretty Coupé was the very first of the purpose-built Group B cars, but was conceived before the Quattro broke cover, and was soon rendered obsolete by its rear-drive-only layout. With more than 300bhp from 2.0-litres (the Evolution car had about 330bhp/2.1-litres), at first it was a rally winner where it could get traction, but was always at a disadvantage on low-grip surfaces. Obsolete as early as 1983, Lancia had nothing better to offer until 1985, so it was its front-line car until the end of that season.

Lancia Delta S4 – mid engine/four-wheel drive. This, the most serious rival to the Peugeot, was of a similar size, with a 450-500bhp output from its 2.0-litre supercharged and turbocharged engine (such a layout had not previously been used in a rally car), and replaced the Rally 037. As expected from Lancia, which was always a very serious rally team, it was a no-holds-barred Group B car, looking like the Delta road car, but almost totally different under the skin. Engineering started after the 205 T16 was announced, and homologation followed in November 1985. A winner at once, and possibly having even more potential than the T16, Henri Toivonen's fatal crash in one (Corsica, May 1986) triggered the cancellation of Group B – and with it, the premature demise of this still under-developed rally car.

MG Metro 6R4 – mid-engine/four-wheel drive. Though it became a clubman's delight in Britain for many years afterwards, as a World rally car the 6R4 was a failure. Austin-Rover's big mistake was to choose a normally-aspirated 3-litre V6 engine (with cylinder heads and detail engineering by Cosworth), whose output was limited to about 420bhp, when rivals with turbocharged engines were already aiming for 600bhp. With a few (very few) panels shared with the Metro family car, its bulges, spoilers and wheel-arch extensions made it pug-ugly. The handling was great, but in just one full World Championship year (1986) it was dismally unreliable. Peugeot was never worried about this car.

Porsche 959 – rear engine/four-wheel drive. This, the most sophisticated of all Group B cars, was developed too slowly, and too thoroughly, which meant that it was not even ready for sale until Group B had been cancelled. Though it was too large and too heavy, the combination of 911 styling, and a racing 956-type engine, with an advanced four-wheel drive system, made it a remarkable prospect, which might eventually have won all round the world. Success in the 1986 Paris-Dakar Raid rally across the Sahara desert proved its worth – but Porsche was interested more in racing than rallying, so Peugeot never had to sweat it out.

Timetable – a tight schedule

Although first thoughts on the form and layout of the car initially coded 'M24-Rally' had been discussed even before Jean Todt took up his new post in October 1981, the actual design and build of the original car came together very rapidly indeed. Here, according to Todt himself, are the important junctures:

December 1981: Peugeot announced that it would tackle a new Group B design

February 1982: The choice of engine – a new-generation four-cylinder XU8T – was made

March 1982: The decision to use a transversely-mounted engine was made

April 1982: The exterior style was settled, and the first mock-up/bodyshell was available

May 1982: The roll cage and other safety features were finalised

June 1982: The interior style of the 200-off 'homologation car' was finally approved

July 1982: Wind tunnel testing to check out exterior and in-body airflows was started

September 1982: First major prototype parts became available

November 1982: Build of the first prototype began

23 February 1983: The first car ran, for the first time, at the Mortefontaine (ex-Chrysler-France, now Peugeot) test track

Homologation – meeting the rules

Although engineering and development then went ahead remarkably smoothly, Peugeot's intention of building cars to the original schedule slipped a little as the enormity of the design job became clear. In the original scheme of things, the car should have been previewed in March 1983, the

Top: This car might look messy, but was, in fact, the original T16 mock-up, in which the basic style and aerodynamic features were being settled in 1982.

Above: This, I believe, shows the build-up of the very first T16 test/prototype car in the winter of 1982/83. Amazingly few changes had to be made after development began.

200 road cars should have been built towards the end of that year, and homologation should have followed on 1 January 1984, so that the team could compete in the Monte Carlo Rally which followed in that month. As we now know, the car did not make its homologated debut until the Tour de Corse in May 1984.

Initially shown at the end of February 1983, it was not nearly ready to go into production. Not only had testing of

This shot shows how the vast rear bodywork of the T16 hinged up from the centre section to allow access to the engine, transmission, and all related running gear. The position of the second spare wheel (which was only occasionally carried) is significant.

Dark blue/grey trim, with red dials, was the theme of the 205 T16 road cars.

The 205 T16's first big win came in the Finnish Lakes of August 1984, when Ari Vatanen and Terry Harryman demolished their opposition.

Ready at last! This was the cutaway drawing of the original T16 on which Peugeot in France and Peugeot-Talbot in the UK had slaved for so long. The basic transverse engine/four-wheel drive layout would be retained for several years, though regular aerodynamic improvements (particularly the arrival of the big-winged E2 of 1985) would often be made.

the single running prototype only just begun (Jean-Pierre Nicolas was the test driver), but the so-called 'car' shown to the press at the time was merely the second prototype, without an engine or most of the transmission in place: the programme was running to as tight a schedule as that.

As Des O'Dell commented at the time: "They have made fantastic progress ... They would only put a small engine into the car first, and they have gradually built up the power to about 305bhp, but there have been no engine problems at all ..."

Because testing went along steadily, rather spectacularly, all hope of entering a prototype in the Mille Pistes rally (July, where non-homologated cars were always welcome) was dashed: in fact, the first works Evolution 1 car was not even completed until August 1983 ... Todt and his bosses, though, wanted to get it right, rather than rush it into the spotlight, risking humiliating results.

Production of the necessary 200-off production run of road cars could not begin until PTS released the specification of the Evolution cars which it wished to take on rallies. As any rally enthusiast knows, it was essential to get the rally car specification right first, so that the de-tuned road cars could have a specification which would not only make changes to the 'Evo' state sporting-legal, but which would also produce a very acceptable road car. By the end of 1983 that aim had been achieved (and, from personal experience of over 500 miles in a road car, I can confirm that the road car was very acceptable indeed!), so slow and patient assembly of the 200bhp road cars, whose two-seater interiors were properly trimmed, with padded and sound-insulated passenger cabins, could then get under way.

To make the process as easy as possible, Peugeot elected to make all the road cars to the same specification, all of them in the same colour, and naturally all of them with left-hand drive. The French body specialists, Heuliez, produced all the structures (using, as their base, standard 205 shells which it then carved about considerably, with the cars being finally assembled in a special facility at the Peugeot (originally Simca/Chrysler-France) factory at Poissy. This was the same assembly line which would eventually produce the 20 modified Evolution cars from which the works fleet of rally cars would evolve.

In March 1984, when the time came for the 205 T16 to be homologated, Peugeot decided to line up every single one of the cars built, on a massive expanse of tarmac so that the FIA inspectors could see for themselves that all the cars truly existed, that no cheating had taken place, and there had been no double-counting of cars to make up the numbers. Homologation was duly granted on 1 April 1984, by which time Peugeot had already laid plans for the car to make its World debut in Corsica on 3 May. The schedule, of course, was tight, but Jean Todt had always planned it that way.

This Peugeot-provided cutaway drawing of the original-type 205 T16 makes the installation of the engine look relatively simple. Not so ...

Engineering features

In the beginning, Jean Todt stated that Talbot's British team boss Des O'Dell would be in overall charge of the project, but within weeks it became clear that this was not going to be the whole and unvarnished outcome. Although O'Dell was to have a team of 15-20 people working under him, this meant that he would have to move to Paris. Tragically, in the next months his wife died, and the devastated O'Dell

Although the new 205 donated the centre section of its shell to the structure of the 205 T16, the remainder was especially designed. This was the original variety, designed in 1982 and revealed in 1983.

had to return to Coventry to resume his British life.

Not only was the new car – the M24-Rally – to be almost entirely French in both concept and engineering, it was also necessary to plan for a run of 200 cars to gain homologation, with the main project work (pre-computerisation, too!) being tackled by project designer Bernard Perron at the PSA research centre at Garenne-Colombes.

Indeed, it was never likely to be otherwise – the French word 'chauvinism' perfectly describes the attitude of Jean Todt, for the little Frenchman was quite determined to see the new car take shape in his native country.

O'Dell and his tiny Coventry-based team, however, had one very important role to play – that until the design was frozen, they could continue to provide an input into practicalities. How quickly could a suspension strut be changed? How difficult would it be to exchange main gearboxes or front and rear differentials in a hurry at a rally service point? If a turbocharger failed (and it would, make no mistake about that, for turbos were not – and still are not – bomb-proof components) would a change be easy? How many different nut and bolt sizes would be needed?

It was this sort of knowledge that Talbot had gained through rally experience, some of it bitter, some of it in the school of hard knocks, and some of it by happy coincidence.

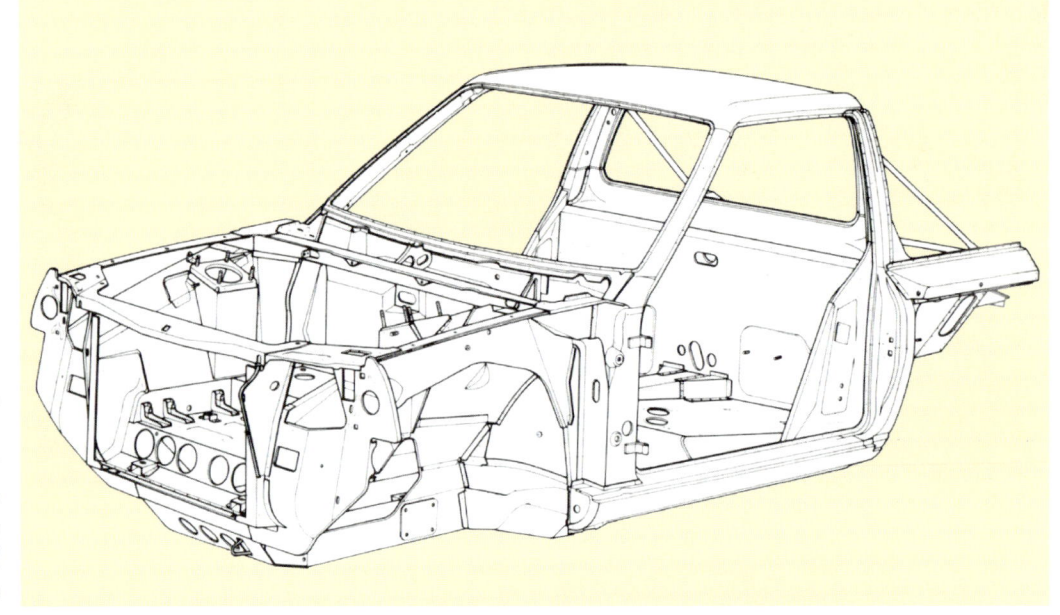

O'Dell's intention was always to influence the design of the car so that it would be as simple as possible, four-wheel drive or not.

Although Peugeot's earlier big, heavy, production-based cars had won several important victories in the late 1970s, Todt could see that a complete change in design thinking was needed. With four-wheel drive now in the ascendant, and Group B about to come into force, he could see that the whole face of rallying was about to change.

Because he not only had a forceful personality (it helped that he had already become a very successful rally co-driver in his own right), and because he had already discovered how to work the 'corridors of power' back at Peugeot HQ, he persuaded the company that they should approve of his vision of what a new Group B should be like.

In effect, and in a remarkably short time, he won approval to develop an all-new Group B car, and to do whatever was needed (and to include whatever engineering features his engineers told him were necessary) to produce an outright winner. Peugeot's directors, for their part, insisted on just one basic factor – that the new car should

The 205 T16's four-wheel drive transmission was made more complicated by the transverse positioning of the engine and main gearbox. The torque-splitting centre differential and viscous coupling were located behind the line of the engine/gearbox. Note that all four outer driveshafts were identical components.

look, superficially at least, like one of the company's mass-production machines. And so it was. Although the hidden technical detail of the car – one which was originally coded the M24-Rally (the mass-market 205 was coded as M24) – was brand new, in its basic style the new rally car was visually close to the latest mass-production Peugeot project, which was due to be launched in 1983 as the Peugeot 205. In mass-market form this was to be a smartly-styled, relatively-conventional, small-medium hatchback, with either three-doors or five-doors. There would be a choice of engines – petrol or diesel, very underpowered and sporting – all of them mounted transversely across the front engine bay, and driving the front wheels.

Accordingly, the profile, basic silhouette and somehow the character of the M24-Rally were closely influenced by the 205, the result being that all of the 200-off production run were pretty little cars which would prove to be surprisingly flexible and 'driver-friendly'.

However, although it must have been a real pleasure for the French design engineers to work on a single-purpose Group B project with so few compromises, it must also have been a little frustrating – cramping even – for them to have to fit everything within the same basic 'package' as the mass-production 205. Furthermore, although this project was still top-secret when 205 T16 work began, it must always have been clear that there would be an enormous spin-off if the mass-market car and the rally car could look so similar, and be launched at the same time. As we now know, that aim was certainly realised, for both appeared in February 1983, immediately before the prestigious Geneva Motor Show.

Within the marketing confines laid down by top management, however, there were quite a lot of visual differences between the two cars. The basic statistics of the front-engined, front-wheel drive, mass-production car included a wheelbase of 7ft 11.3in and an overall width of just 5ft 1.5in, whereas the wheelbase of the 200-off rally car would be 8ft 4in and its width was 5ft 6in.

If the cars were viewed separately, they looked remarkably similar to each other – and certainly gave the two-peas-from-the-same-pod impression – but when placed side-by-side there were many obvious differences, for the rally car was not only larger, but it had a large hot-air outlet above the front radiator, and functional fresh air scoops in the flanks ahead of the rear wheels. However, it was only when inspected, side-by-side and together, that the stretching in wheelbase, overall length, and width became clear.

Even so, there is evidence that the imposed requirement that the team had to use the same basic silhouette and proportions of the new 205 model may have compromised the layout of the rally car to some extent. Peugeot would never admit this, but several other eminent engineers raised their eyebrows when they saw the location of some major and heavy components.

This applied especially to the basic location of the engine, which was set across the car rather than in line with the direction of motion: It did not help that, at first, there was one school of thought which suggested that motive power should be by the normally-aspirated PRV V6 engine, of the type already found in cars as diverse as the Peugeot 604, the Renault 30, the Alpine A610 and the DeLorean DMC12. Des O'Dell was a great proponent of normally-aspirated engines, but in this case this 2.85-litre engine's bulk, and its rather limited reputation for 'tuneability', ruled it out.

Even with a four-cylinder engine chosen, and although clever detail design meant that there were really no more power-sapping gears to be accommodated (the 'centre differential' also turned the drive through ninety degrees – clever), the heavy engine was well to one side of the longitudinal centre line, so its mass could not be totally balanced by any other component, though since left-hand

Coded XU8T, the 205 T16's 1.8-litre turbocharged engine had its own special design of 16-valve cylinder head.

drive was standard (and right-hand drive cars were never envisaged) this was not extreme.

It was the layout of the engine, the main transmission and the four-wheel drive system which were most intriguing. The engineers had certainly pushed their technical freedoms to the limit while keeping everything hidden away under a conventional-looking skin. On the other hand, the steering, suspension and braking installations were all straightforward

Peugeot's new M24 project

It was as early as 1977 that Peugeot's top management started work on 'M24', the range of cars which would eventually become known as the 205. For this car there was a clear and simple objective. Although there would be an overlap on the assembly lines (as is the way of these things), M24 was meant to fill a large gap in the existing project range, to replace the top-of-the-line 104s, and the mid-range 305. This was to be achieved with one basic new structure (to be produced in three-door and five-door varieties), which would use a number of common major parts, all of which were available, or planned by the parent company, PSA.

In particular, each and every M24 (205) would have a front, transversely-mounted four-cylinder engine which drove the front wheels, either the existing small unit which spanned 900cc to 1400cc, or the still-to-be-finalised XU series, which would span 1.5- to 2.0-litres. Not only that, but to suit these engines and their layouts (the small engine, for instance was designed to lie back, almost horizontally, in the engine bay) the under-bonnet package had to accommodate both an under-the-engine transmission, or an 'end-on' transmission. Furthermore, the entire structural package would have to deal with horsepower ratings as low as 45bhp, and as high as 130bhp. As we now know, all those objectives were achieved, with the mainstream 205 range going on sale in the first half of 1983.

enough, and even a proportion of the bodyshell was retained from the three-door version of the mass-production 205 structure.

Todt, the pragmatist, had taken a good look at the then all-conquering Audi Quattro, and the immediately-obsolete Talbot Sunbeam-Lotus before settling on the basics of the new Peugeot. The simple Sunbeam-Lotus rally car had enjoyed about 240bhp, in a car weighing only 2240lb, whereas the original Quattro had 340bhp, and weighed about 2700lb. He must have guessed that Audi was ambitious enough to propose an evolution/Group B version of that car, too – and when it appeared, this would be the 400bhp/Sport Quattro, which also weighed about 2600lb.

Accordingly, he must have realised that by the time the new Peugeot could get into motorsport in 1984, it would need at least 350bhp, and perhaps 400bhp, when the next series of evolution examples came along; for Peugeot that provided a real challenge. As far as the public was concerned, none of the group's normally-aspirated engines looked as if they had anything like that sort of potential locked away, and even if they were to be power-tuned with turbochargers, it was not at all certain that such figures could be available.

The comparison with teams such as Ford was stark. When Ford required 350/400bhp for its new rally cars for the 1980s, it already had a great basic engine on which to work – the Cosworth-designed 16-valve BD family – for which a great deal of turbocharging knowledge was already available, notably with the racing Capris produced by Zakspeed. In Ford's case, it was not a case of "can we?", but of "how far should we go?".

By looking carefully at the Group B regulations, which had just come into force, even before making his recommendations Todt could also juggle with engine sizes (which, according to the new Group B regulations, were deemed to be multiplied by a 'factor' of 1.4 when turbocharged) against minimum car limits. It did not take him long, apparently, to decide that a newly-developed engine should measure no more than 1786cc (or a nominal 2500cc when turbocharged). If this engine was to produce up to 400bhp (and, who knows, maybe more as time passed), its cylinder block would need to be very sturdy, so that it could accept, and deal with, the very substantial compression pressures conferred by turbocharger boost.

If Peugeot/Citroën had not already been developing a new range of four-cylinder engines – the all-new XU family,

The engine of the 205 T16 was mounted behind the passenger seat on the right side of the car.

which were (quite coincidentally) due to make their debut before the end of 1982 – when the 205 T16 was being designed – its chief project engineer, Bernard Perron, and his associate Jean-Claude Vaucard, might have been faced with some unpalatable choices.

The 104-type engine, which was already due to be used in the Citroën 1000 Pistes Group B car, was at once too small, and its configuration and layout in the car, with a transmission built in under its cylinder block, was all wrong. The rest of the company's engines, four-cylinder or V6, were too heavy, too bulky, and were generally an uninspiring bunch.

Fortunately for Todt and his team, the new XU family seemed to be a very promising basis for development. Not only would it immediately be available in 1.6-litre and 1.9-litre sizes (and it was already known, by the way, that it could be squeezed up to a full 2.0-litres in due course), but it had a very sturdy cylinder block and bottom end, with a bore of 83mm and a stroke of 88mm in 1.9-litre form. This looked like a very good way to start, and in the event

Whether the T16 in question was of the original or E2 variety (this was an E2), Peugeot tried to make it easy to gain access to the engine, for there was a removable body panel ahead of the right-side rear wheel.

it was to form the basis of a great new rally engine. Thus it was that a specific derivative, internally coded XU8T (T = turbocharged) was born.

Because the basic availability and dimensions of an engine were now known (even though there was still a long way to go to turn the good idea into reality), the very heart of the new car – its transmission and drive lines – could now be laid out. Even though Talbot rally boss Des O'Dell would later be air-brushed out of the 205 T16's official history, he was much involved in what followed.

Although there was never any doubt that the car would have four-wheel drive (once the Audi Quattro had started winning events it was clear that two-wheel drive cars had been rendered obsolete), and equally little doubt that the engine would be placed behind the two seats, there was much discussion (what other engineers sometimes call the "why don't we ...?" period) about the position of the engine, and the way the transmission would relate to it.

Rather than being in line with the chassis, the engine and main gearbox assemblies were eventually placed transversely, approximately where the rear seats would be located in the normal four-seater front-drive Peugeot

29

205, and in this location were placed behind a vertical bulkhead located immediately behind the passenger seats. The engine was totally to the right side of the car (behind the left-hand drive co-driver's seat), while the main gearbox was all on the left side of the car. I am sure that one major reason behind this was that it allowed an existing Peugeot-Citroën main gearbox to be used.

It had not always been like this. As Jean Todt himself, along with co-author Jean-Louis Moncet, had written in their personal study of the 205 T16 project (*Peugeot 205 – The Story of a Challenge*): "The first design of the M24-Rally showed the engine in a central, longitudinal position. Another design showed it to the right, at the back, off centre. Des O'Dell offered a strong argument for the second possibility. In a rally car there is one part of the engine that cannot be altered: the side on which all the transmission belts (distribution, alternator, pumps) are mounted. This side must, without question, remain accessible. Right, at the back, would be an ideal spot ...

"In March 1982 the engine defined itself as a central rear transverse, offset to the right, with access to the transmission belts via a quickly removable body panel [on the outer skin of the car] in front of the right rear wheel ..."

It transpired that the entire transmission layout had revolved around the availability of a five-speed, two-shaft, all-indirect gearbox which already existed in the Peugeot-Citroën 'parts bin', and is easily recognisable to all PSA classic and motoring enthusiasts. It was that normally found (in an entirely different location, ahead of the front wheels) in the front-wheel drive Citroën SM.

The importance of this transmission is not merely that it was very strong, and suitable, but that it was already available. It is no exaggeration to suggest that much money, and months of design and development, were saved because a new main transmission did not have to be designed for the new rally car.

Incidentally, this SM gearbox already had a lengthy and distinguished history. Not only was it originally conceived for the higher-powered versions of the front-wheel drive Citroën DS of the 1960s, but in the 1970s it also found a

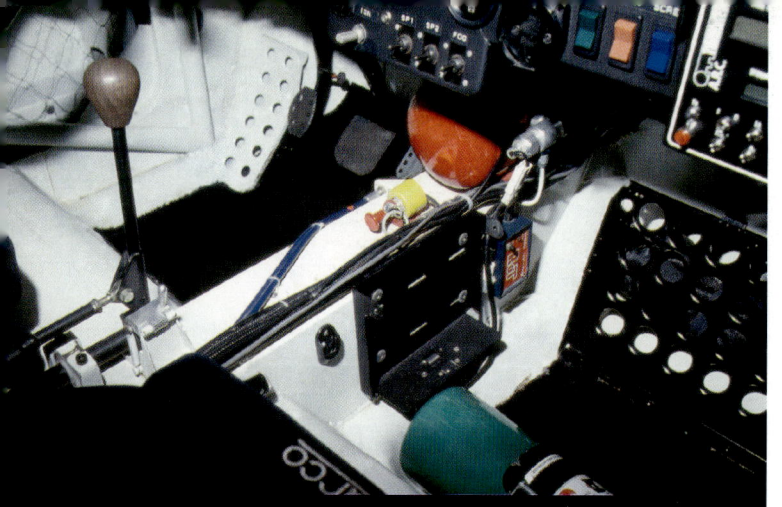

Top: A place for everything in the front seat area ... completion of this early-type T16, in the French workshops, is close. The gear linkage points backwards towards the much-modified Citroën-style transmission which was positioned neatly behind the driver's seat. Above: Laid out on the workshop floor for inspection by the technical press in February 1983, this shows the 205 T16's four-wheel drive layout. The main five-speed gearbox was an adaptation of the existing Citroën SM/Lotus Esprit Turbo transmission, the rest being entirely special.

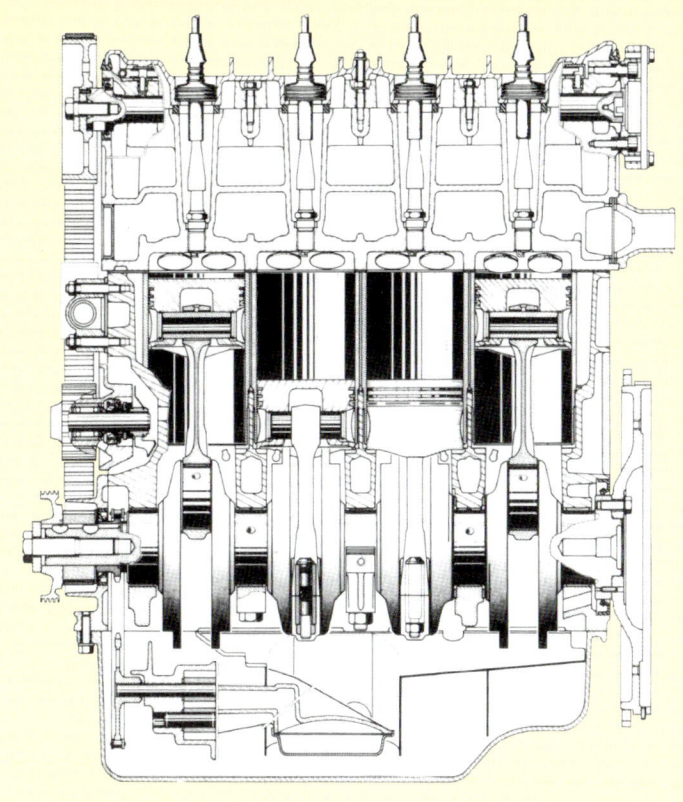

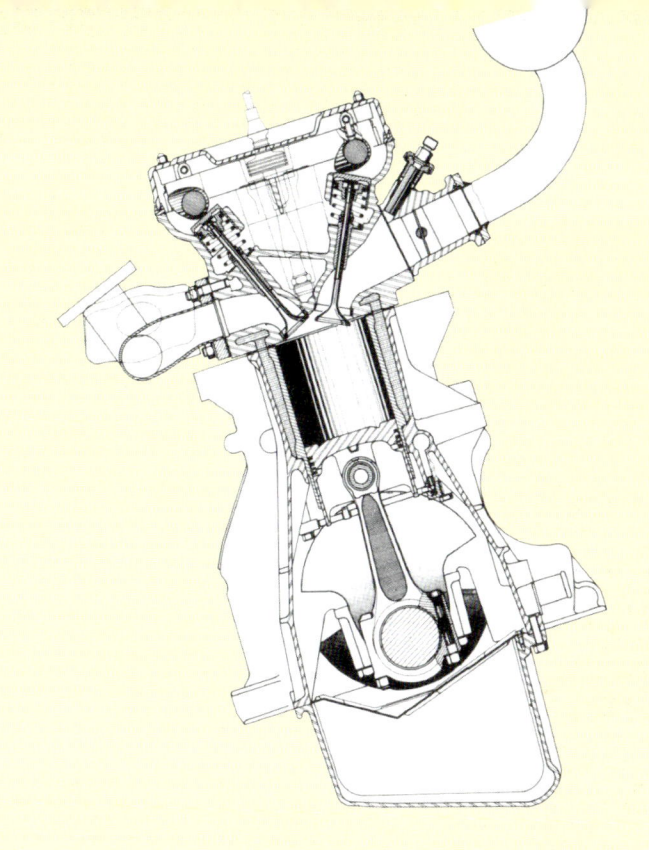

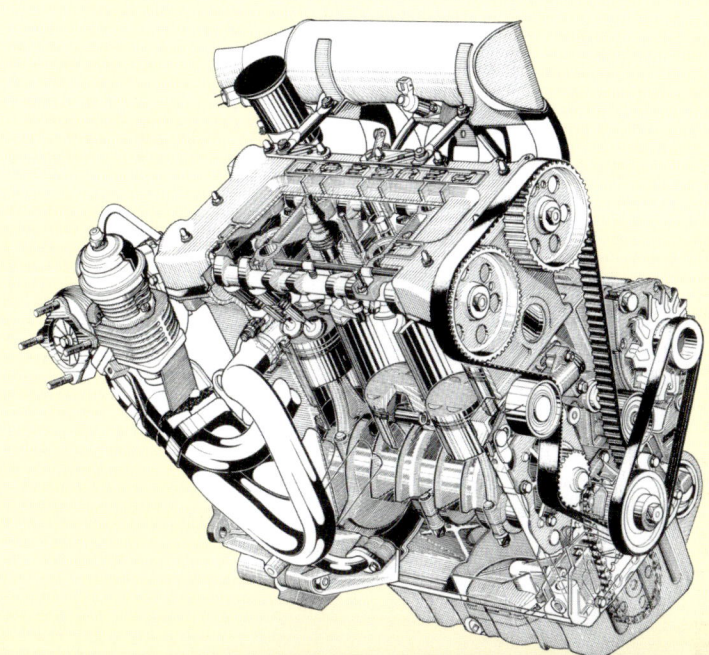

Although the 205 T16's engine used a lightly-modified Type XU diesel cylinder block, the remainder of this turbocharged, narrow-angle, 16-valve engine was designed especially for the rally car. Road cars produced 200bhp; definitive rally cars up to 450bhp.

home, in one derivative or another, in the Maserati Merak, the Lotus Esprit and Esprit Turbo sports Coupés, and also in the mundane Citroën C35 commercial vehicle. Incidentally, it was also soon to find yet another home – which was to form the main gearbox of the desperately unsuccessful Citroën BX 4TC four-wheel drive rally car.

As will become clear from the drawing published on page 25, drive from the engine therefore came in to the top, primary shaft, and left the gearbox where, on the centre line of the car, the drive was turned through 90 degrees by a simple pair of gears, with propeller shafts leading to the front and rear, and to their final drives.

The centre differential (which was actually located immediately behind the line of the main engine/gearbox axis) was an FF Developments epicyclic gear design, complete with viscous coupling. FFD, of course, currently had a monopoly (and the appropriate patents!) on such a layout, which was also to be found in British Group B cars such as the Ford RS200 and the MG Metro 6R4. Like all other such versions of this design, the VC could readily be swapped by replacement differentials to provide a different split of torque between front and rear. In fact, when Peugeot eventually announced the car in the first months of 1983, it mentioned extremes of 25/75 (most of the drive, therefore going to the rear wheels – this was thought to be essential for tarmac stages), and 50/50, with other torque splits also apparently being under development: in fact, when the car was originally homologated, a 33/67 split for gravel was also approved.

Although they were all housed in their own separate, light-alloy castings, the engine, main gearbox, 90-degree turn of drive, centre differential and rear final drive assemblies were then bolted up together to form one massive assembly in the centre/rear of the car. In fact when the 205 T16 was initially released, it had a conventional ZF bevel gear type of limited-slip differential fitted.

This very solid and (frankly) heavy block of machinery was then connected to the front differential/final drive by a large diameter alloy torque tube, with the front differential either having no limited-slip bias at all, or a ZF LSD, for development was still proceeding: in the end, ZF LSDs were standardised at front and rear.

An interesting detail which was often ignored in technical analyses of the car when it was new, was that all four final driveshafts (from the differentials to the wheels) were identical – front and rear, left and right. Not only did this make good engineering sense, but in future it would help the spares provisioning for service vehicles.

I have deliberately not described the engine before analysing the transmission, simply because that was the way in which development of the car's design proceeded. There was really no point in finalising the engine until the engineers knew just where, and how, it was to be installed in the car.

When the original, new generation, mass-production XU engine was introduced in the autumn of 1982, it was seen to have an aluminium cylinder block, with 'wet' pressed-fit cast iron cylinder liners, and an aluminium cylinder head with a line of two valves per cylinder, and a single overhead camshaft, driven by a cogged belt. Two sizes were immediately available, and to flag up the way that the XU8T rally car engine was developed from them, this little chart of the first engines tells its own story:

Type	Bore x stroke	Capacity
XU5	83 x 73mm	1580cc
XU8T	83 x 82mm	1775cc
XU9	83 x 88mm	1905cc

The base engine was set up to be built in enormous quantities, both as a petrol and (with a beefed up cylinder block and a different cylinder head) a diesel power unit, this being produced at Tremery, in Lorraine, in Eastern France.

Once it had been decided to evolve a high-output rally car engine from the basis of the XU engine, the conversion was swiftly, and very competently, achieved. Although the same basic, and known-to-be-robust, five-bearing bottom end was retained (the block was based on that which would be fitted to diesel engines), as was the internally cogged belt camshaft drive, the Peugeot-Talbot design team then

FF Developments – four-wheel drive specialists

Way back in 1950, when tractor tycoon Harry Ferguson had already made his millions from agricultural vehicles and equipment, he was persuaded to set up Harry Ferguson Research, which soon based itself in Coventry. Led by Major Tony Rolt, and with maverick ex-racing driver Freddie Dixon as a supporting character until the mid-1950s, this business began to develop advanced vehicle technologies, particularly four-wheel drive and automatic transmissions.

Various prototype road cars (and one single-seater Coventry-Climax-engined race car, the P99) were built, after which the company began to refine a four-wheel drive conversion for normal front-engine/rear-drive cars which could be applied to many different cars. It was this system which went into cars as diverse as the Ford Capri rallycross specials, the Jensen FF road car, and the BMW 325iX.

Years after the founder died (he died in 1960), Harry Ferguson Research was sold to Tony Rolt and his own backers, and in 1971 it was re-named FF Developments (FF being the 'Ferguson Formula' whose transmission patents were making the company famous). FFD came to concentrate more and more on the design, engineering, development and small-scale production of transmissions, differentials, and four-wheel drive systems. It was in this field that it became one of the most pre-eminent concerns in motorsport, and was an obvious point of contact when the 205 T16 came to be developed.

FFD was taken over by the British engineering consultancy, Ricardo, in 1994, and still operates a specialised transmission operation in the Coventry area.

---

produced a new light-alloy cylinder head, complete with twin overhead camshafts and four valves per cylinder, which were narrowly opposed to each other in the approved manner. The same 83mm cylinder bore was retained but, to reduce the engine capacity to 1775cc (or 2485cc when the turbo 'equivalency factor' was taken into consideration), the stroke was reduced to 82mm.

To make it fit most neatly into this chassis (and, remember, the overall size of the package had really been dictated to the PTS team by Peugeot's top management), the engine was to be installed in the car with the block and head leaning back, towards the tail, by 20 degrees. Because of the cross-flow layout the exhaust side of the engine, including the manifolds and the KKK turbocharger, was located at the rear, while the inlet manifolds and Bosch fuel injection system were at the front.

There was, of course, an air-to-air intercooler between the turbocharger and the inlet manifold, located well over to the left side of the car, and close to the fresh air intake from that side of the car. Although the engine oil cooler was located in the tail, the water cooling radiator was wisely located up front, immediately behind the grille. Twin fuel tanks were mounted low (under the passenger seats) and close to the centre of the wheelbase: a clever innovation at the time, it would become normal practice on all such specially-developed rally cars – Group B and, later, World Rally Car – in the years which followed.

When the 205 T16 was originally unveiled, it was well-received, because the combination of PTS engineering and Peugeot styling (with, it must be admitted, some consultancy advice from Pininfarina) had helped to produce a functional-looking rally car which was also graceful. Even though the wheels – much larger than on the mass-production 205, of course – had been pushed out towards the corner of the structure, with large wheelarch cutouts, the provision for a lot of wheel movement, and with flared front and rear wing pressings to suit, the package still looked good. At that time, it is important to note, there were absolutely no obvious aerodynamic aids in the style – and the rally drivers would soon find that these were needed!

A half-assembled 205 T16, photographed in February 1983. This shows the neat packaging of the transverse engine and the difficulty of finding enough space for exhaust silencers. Engine access at service points was by removing a panel in the right side of the bodyshell.

This is how the engine and four-wheel drive transmission of the 205 T16 were neatly packaged under an elegant outer skin.

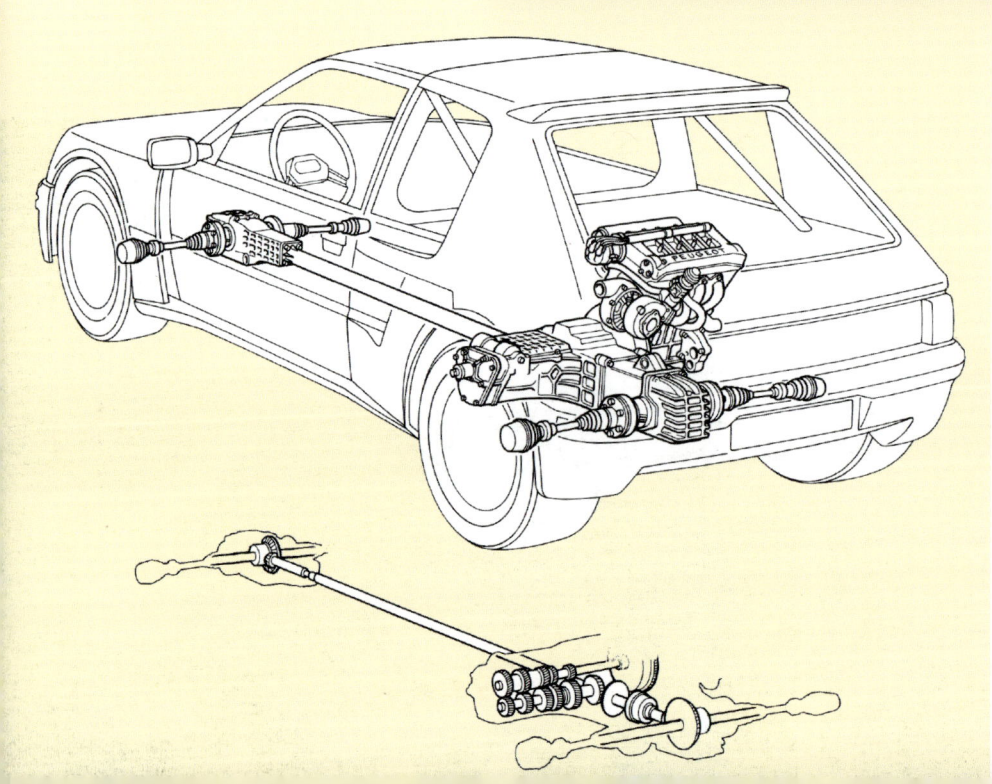

Even so, there was an ongoing anomaly which would never be resolved. More weight was on the right-hand side of the car than the left, the right rear wheel in particular having to carry more load than that on the left. Even so, when it was launched, Peugeot claimed a full-fuel-tank weight of 1145kg/2525lb, of which 54 per cent was carried by the rear wheels.

There were three distinct sections to the monocoque of the new car, a layout which would naturally appear on the entire 220-off production run (though the Second evolution car, described below, would be rather different). The centre section, amazingly, had been based on the standard car's steel shell, though the front was much modified, as

Group B rallying

When the FIA re-shuffled the sporting homologation categories at the end of the 1970s, it proposed that the existing Groups 1, 2, 3 and 4 should be replaced by three new and differently-related categories – Group N, Group A and Group B. Group N ('showroom standard') and Group A required 5000 cars to be built to gain approval, while Group B required only 200 cars to be built. The new groups came into effect in 1982.

Because of the various technical 'freedoms' built into the new categories, and because a build requirement of only 200 was certainly feasible for determined, large-scale, car-makers to consider, Group B attracted a great deal of interest. In the same way that all rally-winning cars of the 1970s tended to be Group 4 (400-off) machines, it became clear that Group B would provide all the winning cars in the mid-1980s.

Because of the numbers involved, it seemed certain that Group B cars could be very special indeed, could (would have to) be expensive, and would be technologically advanced and complex. It soon became clear that any rally-competitive Group B car would need 350-400bhp at first – and by the mid-1980s it was also clear that units producing up to 500bhp would become the norm.

All such good ideas, however, have snags which only become apparent over time. It wasn't long before Audi and Peugeot were joined by Austin-Rover, Citroën, Ford, GM, Lancia, Nissan and Porsche, and once those planners got their teeth into the building of Group B cars it became clear that to build 200 cars (and 20 of the 'evolution' variety which could follow) was a very awkward task.

As one noted project manager once told me: "Any of us can build ten or twenty, we do that by hand – and if the money is there, a million is also feasible, but two hundred, well, that requires some tooling, but not of the permanent variety …"

When launched in February 1983, the 205 T16 had this simple, but rugged, pressed steel structure surrounding the engine position and supporting the rear suspension. All this would change for the E2 model of 1985.

was the rear, which had to accommodate the transversely-positioned engine and the complex four-wheel drive transmission. Naturally, an extremely stout roll cage was integrated into this structure – something for which Ari Vatanen had cause to be thankful when he suffered a high-speed, life-threatening, crash in Argentina in 1985.

For the technical media, there was so much to learn from a study of the transmission and basic drive line layout that the rest of the chassis tended to be ignored. Indeed, by four-wheel drive rally car standards, it was conventional enough, but the details were fascinating. At front and rear, short combined coil-over-shock-absorber struts were used, their upper ends fixing to the structure, their

The independent rear suspension was simply laid out, and all components could be changed very quickly if necessary.

Below: At Des O'Dell's insistence in 1982 and 1983, the T16 shared the same struts (but with different damper settings) at front and rear. This cut service and repair operation times to an absolute minimum.

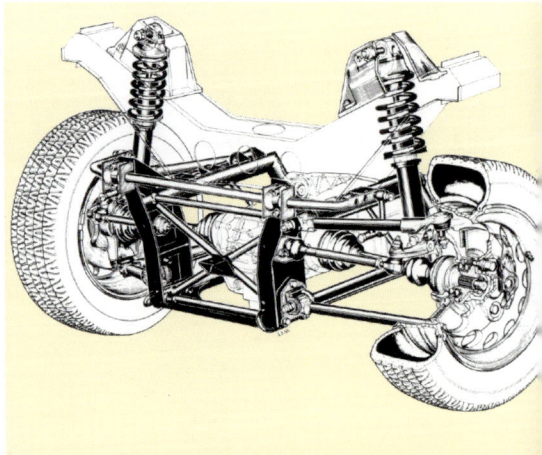

lower ends to the upper wishbones (front) or hub castings (rear).

Once again, Des O'Dell's extensive practical knowledge shone through here, for at his insistence, all the wheel nuts, and retaining nuts for the suspension retaining nuts, and those locating the wishbone fixing pivots were made the same size. In extremis, at the side of the road, in the dark, and – naturally – against the clock – this promised to save a great deal of time – and in the years which followed, it did.

If this all-new design had any flaws (and these would not become obvious for some time), these were that there were no 'add-on' aerodynamic features to trim the high-speed handling. Whereas the Audi Sport Quattro was an aggressive mass of spoilers, the MG Metro 6R4 looked pug-ugly with its enormous rear spoiler, and even the Lancia Rally 037 had a vast rear spoiler to help make it fly straight and level, the 205 T16 was originally a neat, and positively understated, with no more than a minor 'flip' at the top of the rear of the roof to delineate it from the mass-production 205s.

Second evolution car

In motorsport, however, to stand still is to lose ground to one's rivals. On 1 January 1984, an experienced French race engineer, Andre de Cortanze, joined Peugeot as technical director. Once closely involved with the evolution of the Alpine-Renault

The engine bay of the 205 T16 E2 of 1985 and 1986 was impressively full of machinery; this was an extremely reliable and powerful rally car.

When the 205 T16 became 'Evolution 2' in 1985 (left of picture), under engineer de Cortanze's direction there were major changes to the rear-end structure, with a much more powerful engine, and tubes instead of pressings to support the rear suspension.

Below left: What, no silencer? I cannot believe that this particular 205 T16 was ever used on the open road – not, that is, staying within noise limits.

Compared with the original. The E2 type was lightened where possible, made more stable at high speeds, given greater attention to the aerodynamic performance, and provided with more horsepower. Because of the realities of contemporary homologation rules, all these changes were developed in a package, and revealed together. It was typical of Peugeot's resolve that all this work began behind the scenes even before the original car had started its World rallying career.

Although the engine design was still very fresh, the E2 version would be very different from the original, notably with a new cylinder head casting, ports, inlet and exhaust manifolds, a different type of turbocharger (Garrett instead of KKK), a water-cooled instead of an air-cooled intercooler, and electronically controlled water-injection to the engine. All this required greatly improved Bosch K-Jetronic fuel injection/engine management – and a huge amount of testing and development.

Figures later issued by Peugeot show just how much change had been made to the engine in a year: the engine in the original cars, as seen in Corsica in May 1984, developed 335bhp at 7500rpm, but the E2 engine was rated at 424bhp at 7500rpmn – an improvement of no less than 26 per cent made in only a year.

Somehow, too, de Cortanze and his team had pared down the unladen weight of the car from 2073lb to 2007lb. To help do this, the structure of the car had been changed at the rear end, not only to accommodate the revised engine installation, but also to make it more rigid – the moving around of components, radiators, ducting and accessories

cars of the 1970s, he had latterly been working on structural design within Renault.

De Cortanze who, in his own words, knew "0.5 per cent about rallying in 1983", soon saw that the 205 T16 was much more of a pure competition car than earlier rally cars he had known. In effect, he replaced both Des O'Dell (who had been back in the UK for some time), and the Peugeot project design engineers, who had now completed their original layout and schemes. De Cortanze was on board well before the original 205 T16 was homologated – and immediately set about working on a package of changes which would result in the E2 version of the car.

Clockwise from below:

1) No sooner had the 205 T16 been banned from World rallying, than Peugeot re-developed it into the Grand Raid derivative. The original type, as seen here, looked much like the T16 E2, but had an extra section let into the structure, to allow a vast mid-mounted fuel tank to be added.

2) The 405 Grand Raid was a successful off-road/desert/endurance car in its own right, developed directly from the engineering of the 205 T16.

3) According to Peugeot's publicity machine, the 405 T16 Grand Raid was a newly-developed competition car – as, indeed, the styling really was. Much of the running gear, though, was a lineal development from the legendary 205 T16 of the 1980s.

4) As sponsored in major Raid rallies such as Paris-Dakar, the 205 Grand Raid looked purposeful – and was invariably a winner!

5) Spectacular as ever, Ari Vatanen drove a much-modified 205 T16 Grand Raid to win the famous Pikes Peak hillclimb in the USA.

The 205 road car

For many years, the family-owned Peugeot company had made its living by selling millions of family cars – small, small-medium and medium-sized. Small, transverse-engine/front-drive hatchbacks like the 104, 204 and 304 models built up a big and very profitable market share.

To rejuvenate the range in the 1980s, Peugeot elected to develop a new front-wheel drive car to be badged '205', a hatchback which would run on a 93.3in wheelbase, and be built as a three-door or a five-door type. All derivatives (and the choice was, eventually, enormous) had front, transversely-mounted engines and gearboxes, allied to front-wheel drive, the choice of four-cylinder engines eventually spanning 1.0-litre to 1.9-litre (petrol), from 45bhp to 130bhp, with diesel-engined alternatives. Of these 'normal' road cars, the most technically interesting were, of course, the 1.6-litre and 1.9-litre 205 GTi types, which built up their own motorsport reputations at club level.

Except for a strong visual resemblance, and the use of a few standard body parts, there was virtually no direct connection between the normal 205s and the T16 Group B car, but the marketing connection was always close. In fact, the normal 205 had a conventional steel unit-construction bodyshell, MacPherson strut front suspension, and independent rear suspension by trailing arms and transverse torsion bars, none of which had any technical connection with the T16.

Built in several countries, including the UK, the 205 was an enormous success. From 1983 until the late 1990s, when it was finally retired, 5.3 million were produced: these days, of course, it is the 200-off 205 T16 which is remembered most fondly ...

becoming more obvious when the rear body section of the new car was removed and the layout of the 'chassis' could be compared with the old. Most noticeably, tubes replaced box sections between the roll hoop behind the doors to the top of the rear suspension towers.

Visually, too, there was now a large spoiler on the rear of the roof, and a big 'chin spoiler' under the nose (allied to 'splash guards' ahead of the front wheels). Not only did this make the latest car look more dramatic, and sinisterly purposeful, but it also helped it to 'fly' more predictably over high-speed jumps.

All this was just a start to a series of development changes which were applied to the E2 before the end of 1986 (and, if Group B had not been put under sentence of death in mid-season, more changes would certainly have been made.).

Apart from work specifically intended to make the cars stronger and more reliable, there were several aerodynamic tweaks. In particular, the rear of the under-car skid plate was re-shaped to provide a modicum of down-force, while 'side-protection' pieces were added under the floor pan, though they also seemed to have influenced the under-car airflow, too: these were what all the fuss was about on the San Remo Rally, the disturbances being analysed in the 'Competition Story' section of this book.

Not only that, but extra cooling was provided to shock absorbers by the injection of water, an alternative six-speed transmission was used from the Tour de Corse (according to regulations, this could only be homologated one year after the previous change), and for San Remo (where the Lancia Delta S4 was a big rival, experimental high-boost engines produced no less than 540bhp.

Although Todt carried on improving and perfecting the T16 E2s until both the Manufacturers' and Drivers' Championships had been secured, the abruptly enforced cancellation of Group B meant that the car would have no World rallying future in 1987. Accordingly, for a future in desert-racing classics such as the Paris-Dakar, his team rapidly re-developed the chassis. Under Andre de Cortanze, they lengthened the wheelbase of the platform by 11.8in/300mm, thus finding space for an extra long-range petrol tank of 41.9 gallons/190 litres in the newly-generated space between the seats and the engine, keeping the existing low-mounted tanks, thus boosting the total reservoir capacity to no less than 88 gallons/400 litres.

The entire structure was reinforced to take account of the enlarging of the platform, the existing 'Safari' type of suspension was used with modified geometry, front and rear tracks were increased by 4.0in/100mm, and twin spring/shock absorber assemblies were provided at each corner (instead of the single units fitted to normal World rally cars).

The engine itself was slightly detuned – Peugeot claimed only 360bhp/8000rpm, with 2.2 bar of boost, while the gearbox ratios were revised to make the car easier to drive slowly in sand and water (though a very 'long' sixth gear was retained to ensure a high top speed). To keep a clean air intake, the scoops were now re-positioned on the roof, rather than the flanks, of the structure.

This car, the 205 T16 Grand Raid, which weighed no less than 2866lb/1300kg, was made ready at great speed, and ran for the first time on 20 October 1986. Many thousands of testing kilometres had been completed before it even started an event.

Along with the later, re-styled, '405' version which followed it (the looks changed, though the running gear

All works T16s (this is a late model E2) were built so that the entire rear bodywork could be removed in order that the mechanics could get at any part of the running gear. This overhead shot, too, emphasises how short and utterly functional the T16 actually was.

was virtually the same), these cars would be very successful indeed in the late 1980s and early 1990s.

Was the 205 T16 unique?

In the early 1980s, what made the 205 T16 stand out was that it was the very first of the purpose-built four-wheel drive supercars which were to transform the face of rallying in the next few years. Rally car engineering, effectively, was split between 'before Quattro', and 'after Quattro' – with the 205 T16 being the very first, and arguably the most effective, of all the 'after Quattro' models.

Once the sporting authorities had approved the use of four-wheel drive in rallying, Audi only became dominant from 1981 to 1984 because it had virtually stumbled across a cheap and cheerful system for the Quattro, which worked well enough when there were no competent rivals: dominance came about because the Audi team was the only one with such a car at the time.

If the Quattro had been a failure, it would probably have been years before real four-wheel drive rally cars were developed, and indeed other teams (Ford, Lancia and Toyota among them) all designed new Group B models with rear-wheel drive only. It was only when the Quattro – a car which was really an ultra-powerful conversion from front-wheel drive, crudely detailed, unwieldy in its handling, and bombastically run by its management – began to win events, that the opposition began to sit up and take notice.

The Peugeot was unique because it was the very first of a new breed – not a conversion, not a lash-up, but a car totally, correctly and lovingly engineered to take advantage of four-wheel drive. It was unique because it embodied every virtue of a programme undertaken with one aim in mind, and few compromises – victory!

Although the T16 was not quite a ground-up project – the engineers were, at least, constrained by the need to keep a silhouette similar to that of the forthcoming 205 mass-production car – it was the nearest thing to a pure engineering solution to a particular rally car problem that had thus far been attempted, and for that reason it certainly qualifies as unique at the time.

Because work on the T16 began at the end of 1981, and the new car was revealed in March 1983, it easily qualifies as the very first turbocharged, purpose-built, four-wheel drive rally car of all time. Interestingly enough, Lancia's rally team worked to a similar sort of brief, and evolved the Delta S4, but it is significant that they did not start detail design until they had some sort of inspiration – the 205 T16 – on which to draw ...

Building and running the works cars

Not for nothing was Jean Todt known, in certain quarters at Peugeot, as 'Napoleon', for like that great French figure of years gone by, he was a small man with a huge personality, a high opinion of his own status and capabilities, and when running Peugeot-Talbot Sport he always expected to get his own way.

The works team, therefore, ran in the way that he wanted it. He was never short of staff to do his bidding and, by all accounts, his team was never short of funds either. He was, however, lucky in that the car always matched expectations (as did his drivers), and his long term plans – laid in 1982/83 – were carried forward to the end of the Group B era without a hitch.

Although much of the initial design of the T16 was carried out for Todt by Bernard Perron's project team at the PSA research centre at Garenne-Colombes, once the time came to build test cars, and to evolve the team, Todt acquired workshops at rue Paul Bert in Boulogne (not on the Channel coast, but close to Paris). Naturally these workshops did not produce any of the 200 road cars, but in 1983 and 1984 they assembled the 20 original evolution models, while the Evolution 2 (E2) variety) were also produced there. By the time the team was fully established, and rally entries had been made, between 100 and 200 people were working there.

A look at panoramic pictures shows that PTS had plenty of space in which to work – far more, for instance, than Des O'Dell had ever enjoyed at Talbot in Coventry and at least five times the floor area of the otherwise well-equipped Ford Motorsport premises at Boreham in Essex. The difference,

One way to get at the engine bay of the 205 T16 E2 was to take off the entire rear end of the bodywork, and climb in from above! Among the onlookers are engineer Andre de Cortanze (immediately to the right, as we see it, of the camera lens), and Jean-Pierre 'Jumbo' Nicolas (far left).

A message to its rivals: "Be afraid, be very afraid" – for this was a measure of Peugeot's strength and resolve as the 1985 season opened. Ari Vatanen is standing in front of the front wheel of the 205 T16, and (working left as we see them standing in the front line-up) are Terry Harryman, Bruno Saby, Timo Salonen, Jean Todt, Seppo Harjanne, Jean-Francois Fauchille and Jean-Pierre Nicolas.

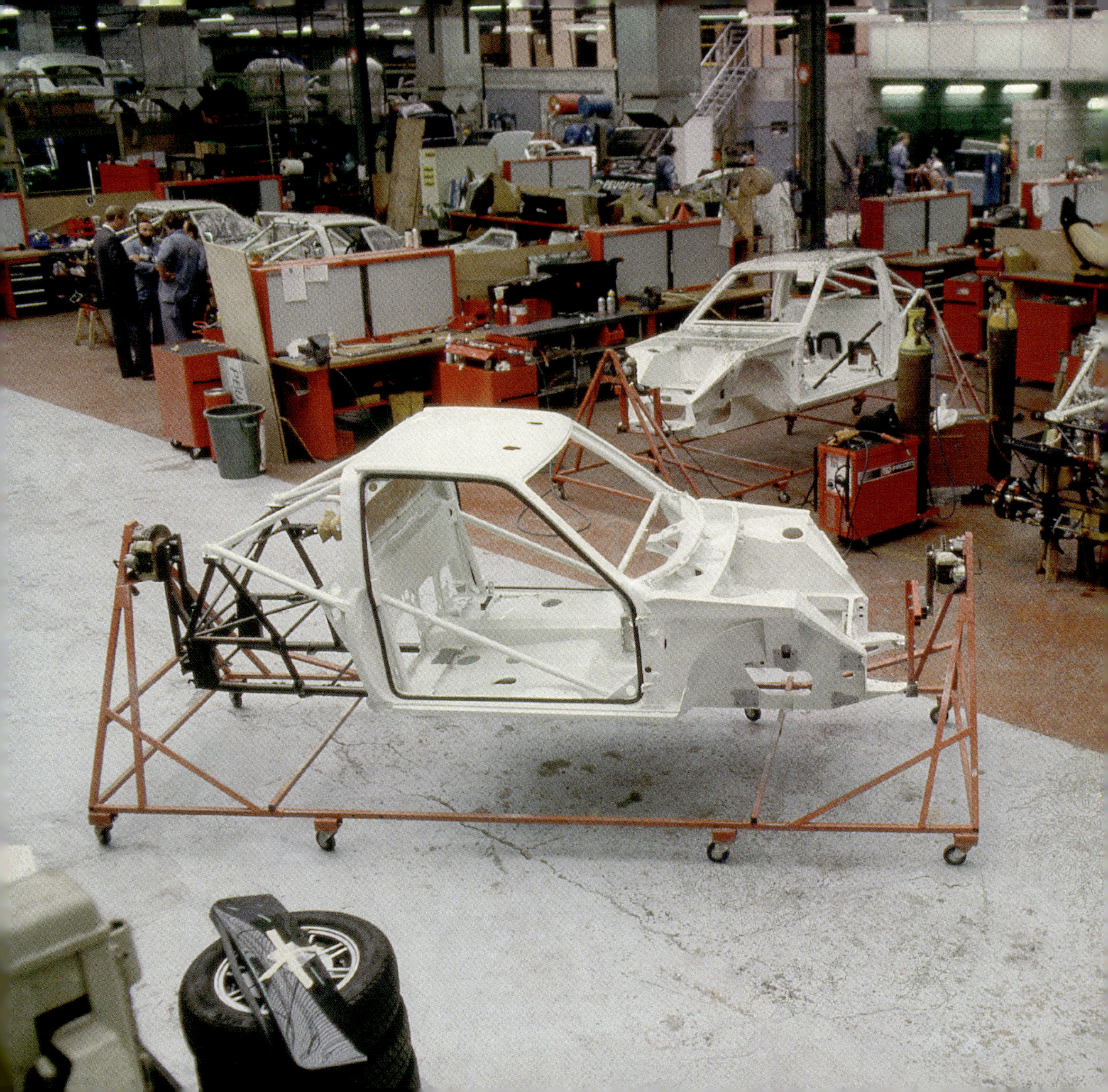

however, was that Todt's Peugeot team carried out much more of their own preparation, rather than sub-contracting out some of the effort in the Ford manner.

Intensive use of cars

Unlike, say, Lancia, which often sold off a works car after one or two events (selling, too, at inflated prices so that the team could raise more funds), Peugeot carried on using its Group B cars as long as they were solid and serviceable. In those days, don't forget, practice for an event meant just that – practice – and not low-speed surveys, so a car's usage tended to follow the typical works pattern – new rally car, nearly-new rally car, practice car, test car, sell-off to private owner.

Of the first twenty examples, several newly-built E1 cars were sold direct to favoured customers – C13 went off to Peugeot-Germany (for Kalle Grundel to drive) and C20 went to Des O'Dell in the UK for Michael Sundstrom, both of them for 1985.

Although the team showed off 20 apparently-complete 'evolution' cars in March 1984, to gain Group B homologation, by no means all them were finished off, nor were they ready to run. At first, indeed, there was more space than cars in the PTS workshops, as Peugeot's meticulously kept records prove. Only a single test car was ready before the summer of 1983, after which the very first evolution test car also ran. By the time that rally cars were commissioned in 1984, five prototypes had also been constructed.

By the end of 1984, the first seven rally cars (C1-C7) had been used on events themselves, two test/development cars had also been used for tests/practice, and three cars (C2, C3 and C5) had already been allocated to practice duties.

Starting from a yawningly bare workshop, Jean Todt created a spacious and modern works competitions department in France – one which was the envy of all Peugeot's rivals. One can see why. This study dates from 1986, with a series of E2 cars being prepared.

45

The pace quickened in 1985. Not only did the balance of the 'first evolution' cars (C8-C20) make their appearance, but the first four Evolution 2 machines (C201-C204) were all put to use.

With only a single exception (Michele Mouton/Monte Carlo/C13), every car seen in 1986 was an E2 model, the identity of the thirteen numbers spanning C206 to C219, with E2 models also being used extensively in practice and for testing purposes, too.

It would be quite wrong (foolish, even, as some 'cloning' certainly took place) to state firmly how many 205 T16s were ever used by the works team, but even according to the official chassis numbers, that total easily exceeds the 40 suggested by two different runs of Evolution models.

Although pressure eased a little in later years, PTS' resources were under pressure in 1984, especially as Ari Vatanen's original Corsica car (C1) was destroyed by fire on that event, C2 was destroyed in a non-rallying accident, and C3 was also destroyed by fire when testing in East Africa in October 1984.

On the other hand, the first E1 to win a World event – Ari Vatanen's C5 in the 1984 1000 Lakes – had a very busy life. In less than a year it won the 1000 Lakes, was used for practice in San Remo 1984, then used for practice in Monte Carlo, Portugal and Corsica, before being used in back-to-back testing (Jean-Pierre Jabouille was the driver) against an early E2 model (C201) at the Michelin test tracks at Clermont Ferrand. Later in the year it would be used for pre-San Remo 1985 testing, before finally being pensioned off.

Note that although the original 205 Grand Raid test car was constructed by rebuilding one of the existing fleet of T16s, a series of new Grand Raid models was then built for 1987 and beyond.

This study shows how the entire rear bodywork could be lifted to give better access to the transverse mid-engined unit and transmission of the 205 T16.

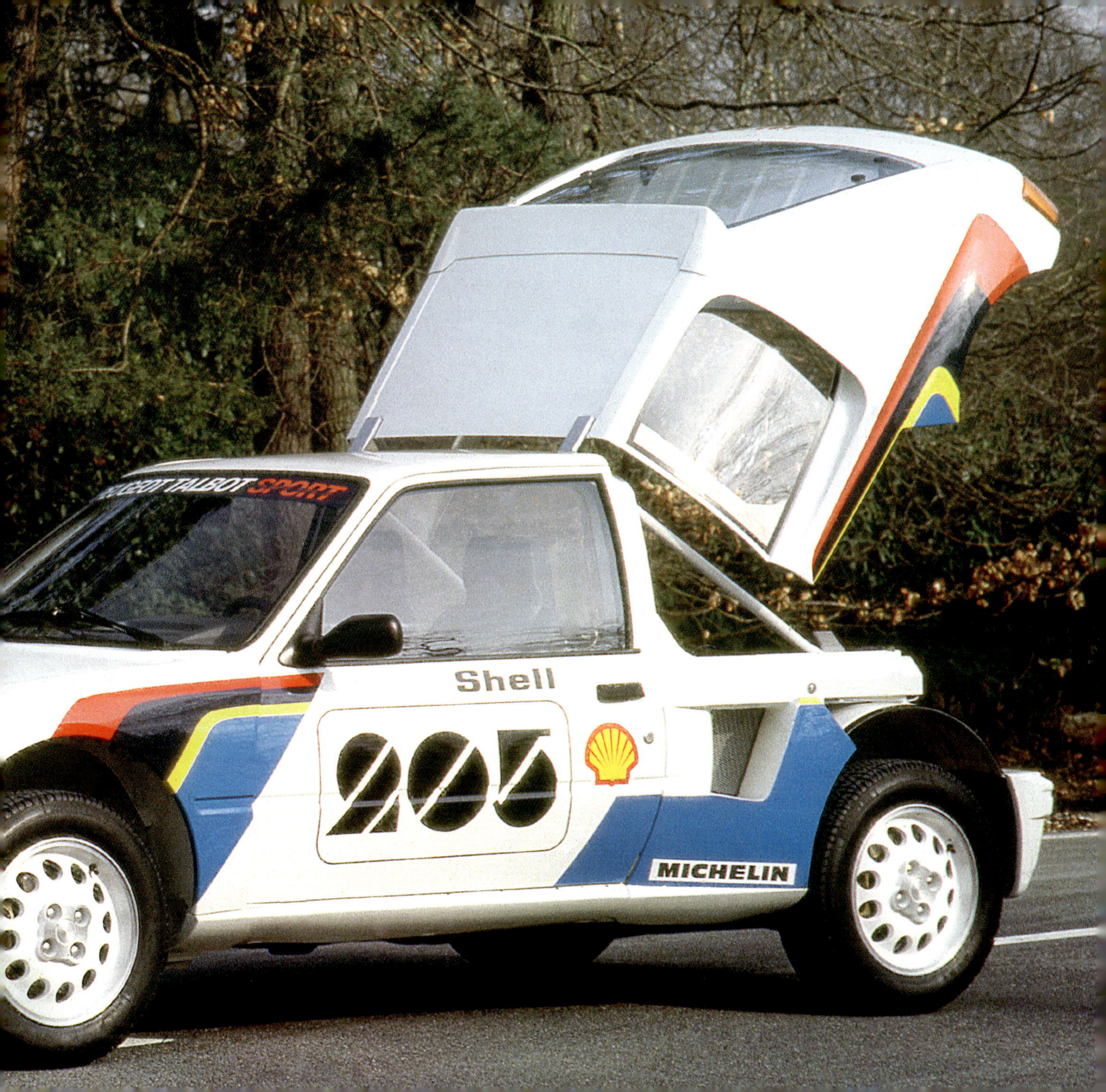
SPORT
Shell
205
MICHELIN

Η ΑΓΡΟΤΙΚΗ
ΑΣΦΑΛΙΣΤΙΚΗ
ΓΕΝΙΚΕΣ ΚΑΙ ΑΓΡΟΤΙΚΕΣ ΑΣΦΑΛΕΙΕΣ
ΑΣΦΑΛΕΙΕΣ ΖΩΗΣ
TALBOT SPORT
Shell
PEUGEOT

Neat and understated – very understated – is the grouping of a three T16 team entry. With only one service van and one management car in sight, there must be an entire fleet of support vehicles out of range of the cameras!

A scene from the Acropolis rally of 1986, Juha Kankkunen won in car number 5.

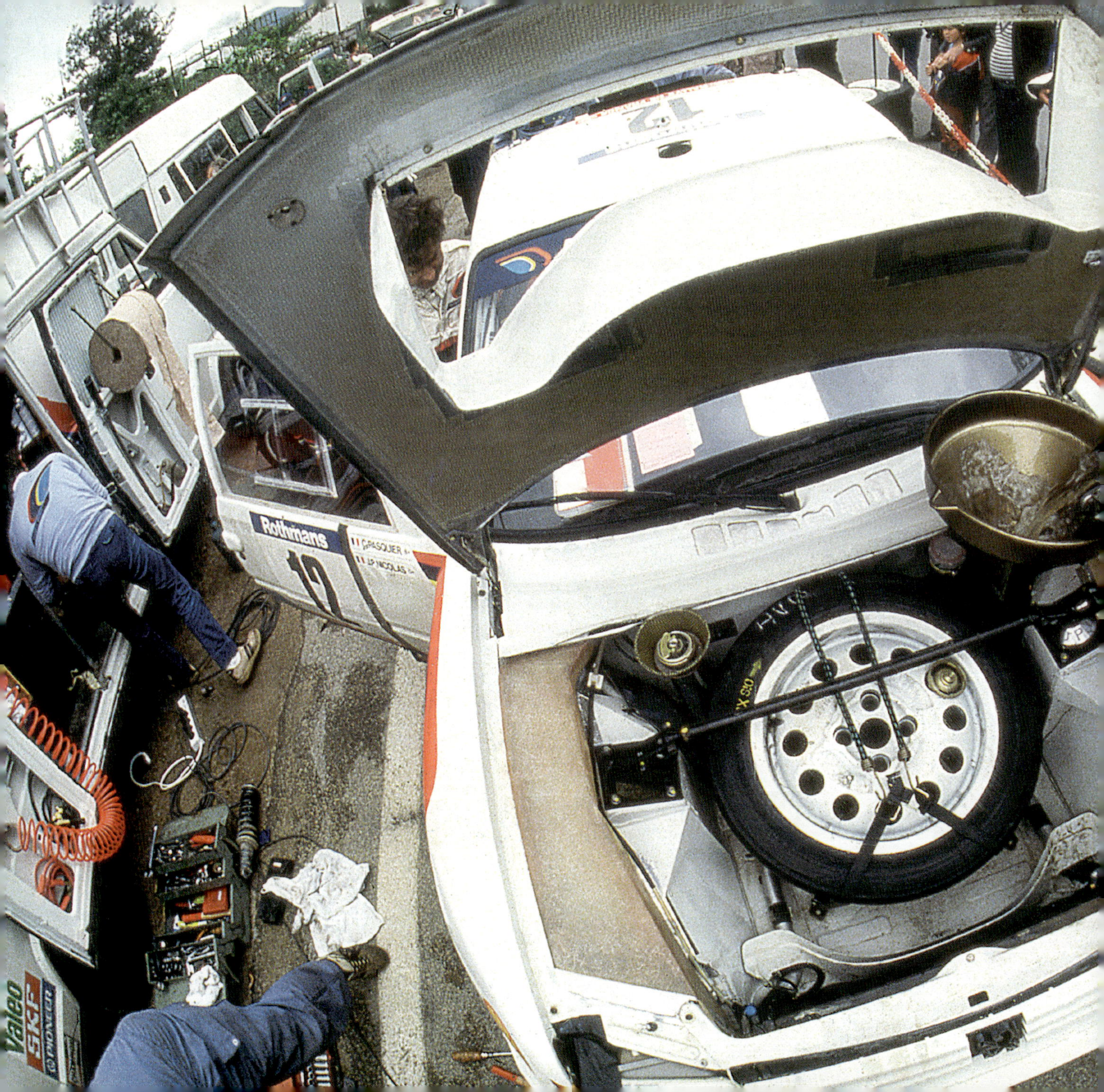
Rothmans
Valeo
SKF

Left: Surprisingly little of the T16's running gear was located up front, as this service shot confirms. The front differential, of course, is hidden away under the spare wheel.

No rush to service this E2, seen at a service point on the Lombard RAC Rally of 1985, with Timo Salonen on his way to a hard-fought victory.

It wasn't always high-tech in a T16 service area! Somewhere in there is a works T16, but the rear body work is being held open by nothing more complicated than a ladder!

A place for everything. When Jean Todt and Des O'Dell were planning this new programme, they made sure that dedicated service/support vans were ideally equipped for their purpose. Nothing so tidy and accessible had previously been seen on the World Championship rally circuit.

Personalities and star drivers
Jean Todt

Like many enthusiastic young Frenchmen, Jean Todt originally wanted to be a race and rally-winning driver, it was only the usual problems – a chronic shortage of funds, and the growing realisation that he was not perhaps as talented as some of his rivals – which caused him to accept the alternative: to be a co-driver instead. It was typical of the young Todt's determination, and application, that he soon became supreme, the best in France and (some said) the best in the whole of Europe.

Born in Pierrefort in 1946, the son of a Polish doctor, Jean Todt started out in motor racing when he was 18, rapidly ran out of money and cars, and resumed as a co-driver in 1966. By 1968 he had broken into works teams, first with Renault, then Ford-France and, from 1970, with Peugeot.

Little by little, he gained influence in the very modest Peugeot team, gaining credibility by attracting 'guest' drivers like Hannu Mikkola, Timo Makinen and Simo Lampinen to drive the company's cars in rallies. By the late 1970s he was certainly the single most important individual

Jean Todt, already an internationally-renowned rally co-driver, became Peugeot's team chief in 1981, and guided the 205 T16 through all the successes of 1984–1986.

in the team, and invariably occupied a co-driver's seat on every event. By 1980 he was also in the (Peugeot-owned) Talbot World rally team – and, in October 1981, he took over the management of the ambitiously expanded team in France.

One of his most decisive actions was to recommend killing-off the Talbot F1 operation (which was not a success), and to begin building Peugeot into a serious World-winning rally team. The result of this, of course, was the launch of the 205 T16 in 1984.

For the next decade and more, everything that happened in Peugeot's motorsport operation was directed by Todt, who took the 205 T16 to the top of the tree, then followed it up with the 'Grand Raid' versions and the 405 T16 which dominated events like the Paris-Dakar rallies, and the North American Pike's Peak hillclimb, of the late 1980s.

Not that this was enough for the ambitious little Frenchman, who then saw Peugeot enter sportscar racing with the Le Mans winning 905s, after which he was also instrumental in making developed versions of that car's V10 engines available for F1 cars.

When Ferrari set out to revitalise its own F1 team effort, Todt was attracted to run the team. Having joined Ferrari in 1993, he assembled a world-beating team around him, including, of course, Michael Schumacher, and in the early 2000s he was put in charge of all Ferrari activities – not merely the racing team – in Italy.

Des O'Dell

Des O'Dell's part in developing the 205 T16 has occasionally been overlooked, not least because he was a Briton working among the chauvinistic French (who wanted to claim all the M24-Rally programme as their own), and because his part in the programme came to an end before it was publicly revealed. Yet Des, as manager of the Talbot Sunbeam-Lotus team which won the World Rally Championship for Makes in 1981, had offered an amazing amount of practical input to the layout of this phenomenal little car.

Born in 1927, Des first got involved in motorsport as

Peugeot-Talbot's team boss behind the effort which delivered the 1981 World Rally Championship for Makes was Des O'Dell, who gave invaluable advice when the new 205 T16 was being engineered.

55

PARIS
2
MICHELIN
A.VATANEN
T.HARRYMAN
Valeo
BILSTEIN
speedline
SKF

a mechanic with the Aston Martin racing sportscars of the late 1950s, and later worked on the original Ford GT40 race cars in 1964 and 1965. The then newly-appointed team manager of the Rootes Group motorsport operation, Marcus Chambers (who needed help with the Ford V8 engines used in his Sunbeam Tigers), hired him to work in Coventry as his technical assistant. Before long, the ever-practical O'Dell became the de facto rally engineer, and when Marcus moved on in 1969, he became the Competitions Manager.

In the next two, often turbulent, decades, Des ran the Rootes (which became Chrysler-UK, which became Talbot) motorsport operations, running a variety of race and rally cars. Notable successes included Avengers, which won touring car races, and of course the Talbot Sunbeam-Lotus which won the World Rally Championship, but a notable failure was the Avenger-BRM, where the Lincolnshire-based race team's four-cylinder engine was a dismal flop, unable to match the phenomenal Ford-Cosworth BDA power unit in the Escort.

Even after the centre of gravity of the motorsport team moved from Britain to France, Des' operation in Coventry carried on, backed by his great enthusiasm, especially for clubmen, and for the cars they were driving. Des died in 1999.

Ari Vatanen

The Finnish star Ari Vatanen was, and still is, every rally enthusiast's hero for, in an action-packed rally career he not only combined unearthly driving skills with great successes and near-death encounters in crashes, but also had blond good looks, infectious friendliness, and great charisma. First seen in World rallying in 1975, he was still competitive two full decades later.

Peugeot's dynamic duo of 1984 and 1985 were driver Ari Vatanen (right) and co-driver Terry Harryman. They recorded the 205 T16's first-ever World victory in the 1984 1000 Lakes, won the Monte of 1985 (this picture), and went on to make it five outright victories in consecutive events.

Born in Joensuu, Finland, in 1952, Ari started rallying in disgracefully scruffy Opel Asconas, and burst on to the World stage in works Ford Escorts in 1975. Always rapid, and invariably successful if he did not crash his cars, he won his first World event (Acropolis) in 1980, then the World Driver's Championship in Rothmans-sponsored Escorts in 1981.

After a relatively unsuccessful 1983 season in Rothmans-sponsored Opels, he joined Peugeot, winning six World rallies in 1984 and 1985. After sustaining serious injuries in a high-speed crash in Argentina in mid-1985, he eventually returned to drive 205 T16 derivatives in 'Raid' rallies, winning the Paris-Dakar classic on several occasions, and the Pike's Peak hillclimb in the USA.

Ari in his prime was one of the most flamboyant of all rally drivers, seemingly without a vestige of fear in his physical and mental make-up. At home on loose surfaces, ice and snow, and on tarmac, he clearly loved the performance which the Peugeot gave him.

In later years he drove for Mitsubishi, Subaru, and again for Ford, but from the late 1990s he entered another stage in his life, becoming a Member of the European Parliament. Although he had been away from active rallying for some years, he still received a rapturous welcome when he appeared at a major historic rallying festival in the UK in 2006.

Jean-Pierre Nicolas

Latterly known as 'Jumbo', or 'Fats' to his friends – both nicknames coming from his rather rotund figure as he reached rallying maturity in the 1970s – 'JPN' had been retired from motorsport for three years before Jean Todt approached him in December 1982 to take on the vitally important testing role for the new 205 T16.

Born and bred in Marseilles, Nicolas had started driving in club events in a Renault 8 Gordini in 1965, and rose to become a works driver for Alpine-Renault by the end of the decade. For the next five years he was faithful to Alpine, winning the Tour de Corse, many European Championship rounds, and being highly-placed on almost every World rally in Europe.

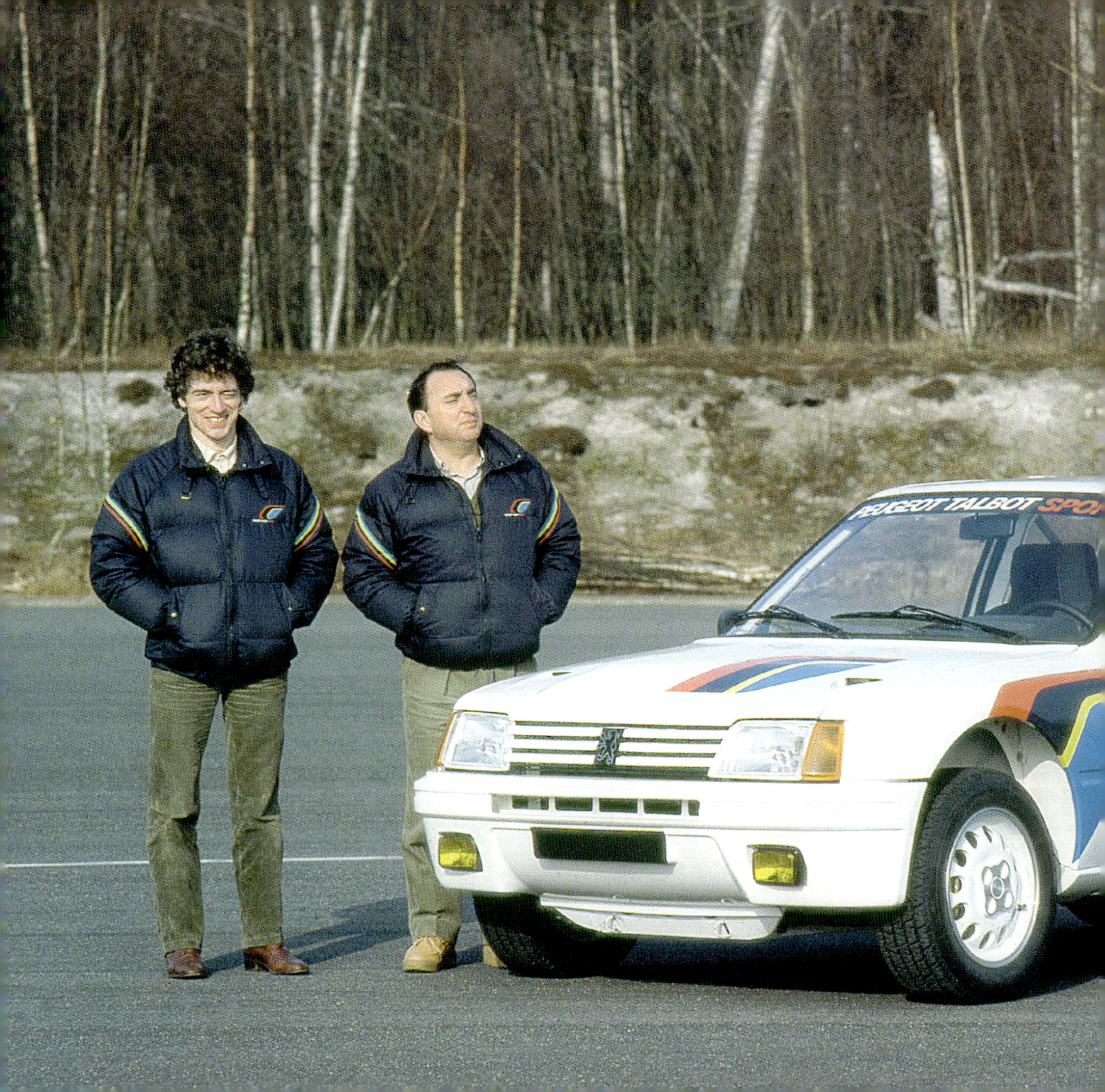
PEUGEOT TALBOT SPO

His first victory for Peugeot came in a 504, in the 1976 Rally of Morocco, but his most astonishing win was in the 1978 Monte, when he drove a privately-prepared Porsche 911 to outright victory after various works cars and teams hit trouble. In 1978 Peugeot was delighted to see JPN drive works 504 V6 Coupés to victory in the two longest and roughest of all rallies – Safari and Bandama/Ivory Coast – before he finally withdrew from motorsport in 1979.

After becoming a commercial sales director in a Renault distributorship in Marseilles, he seemed to be settling in to a placid second career – until the phone call came from Jean Todt in Paris, who had spent many hours alongside him in rally cars over the years. Todt's proposals were that Nicolas should be the team's principal test driver throughout 1983 and the first months of 1984, and that he should become a team driver in 1984.

To quote Todt from his own book about the car: "Despite his 38 years, and vast experience, 'Jumbo' felt like a youngster again."

And so it proved. Although he could not hope to match the amazing performances regularly put up by Ari Vatanen in the lead car in 1984, JPN was the ideal 'anchor man' for such a fast-developing team. At the end of 1984, though, he finally retired from the driving seat, and became head of PTS' Sport Promotion Department instead.

Timo Salonen

Although in so many ways a PR man's nightmare – he was laid back, always wore large spectacles, was rather rotund and a heavy smoker – Timo Salonen was yet another fabulously fast Finnish driver, who might have achieved more if he had tried harder.

In one of the shrewdest moves of his long career, Jean Todt wooed this man, Jean-Pierre Nicolas (right), out of retirement, to head up the test team behind the new 205 T16 rally car project. Nicolas, who had already won the Monte Carlo and Safari rallies in other models, was an ideal choice.

Just one basic statistic tells its own story ... Although he first drove works cars (Fiat 131 Abarths) in 1977, he did not join Peugeot until 1985 – although he had first been spotted by the rallying fraternity in the late 1970s, he spent far too long with uncompetitive Datsun and Nissan teams (contentedly, it seems) before joining Peugeot – instantly becoming World Rally Champion!

Born in Helsinki in 1951, he took up rallying in the 1970s, started his first World Championship event in 1974 (1000 Lakes, of course!), but did not come to prominence until 1977, when he picked up several drives in works Fiat 131 Abarth saloons. On his very first drive with the team – 1000 Lakes – he took second place, and almost immediately went to Canada and won in a similar Fiat.

That, though, was the height of it, for in 1979 he joined the Datsun/Nissan team, racing a series of not-very-

Right: Timo Salonen joined Peugeot for 1985, and became World Rally Champion at the end of that season.

Seppo Harjanne was the taciturn, but supremely efficient Finn who co-drove Timo Salonen through all his successes with Peugeot in 1985 and 1986.

competitive cars, staying until the end of 1984. Placid, and seemingly able to put up with mediocre machinery if the pay was good and if he was properly appreciated, there would be only two victories in those years – in New Zealand in 1980 and in the Ivory Coast in 1981.

By the end of 1984, when he had already been driving normally-aspirated, rear-drive, Nissan 240RS Coupés for two years, a lesser character than Timo would no doubt have been having tantrums and constantly bewailing his ill-fortunes to the media, yet he just kept on, picking up minor placings – his very best being a fortunate second in New Zealand in 1982.

Timo then joined Peugeot though, as he later discovered, only because Jean Todt's negotiations with Walter Rohrl and Markku Alen had both broken down. No matter, for this is what Todt later had to say about him: "He had a beautiful touch at the wheel. Moreover he had firmly mastered a car [the Nissan 240RS] that was not really up to the competition. He was a risk, nevertheless. I had known him to be a little lazy with regard to recce work …"

The record shows just how effective Timo was in his two years with the 205 T16, for in 1985 he won five events – four of them in successive outings – and clinched the World Rally Championship, while in 1986 he won two more rounds, and finished third in the Drivers' series.

When Peugeot turned to Raid rallies, Timo then moved out, to drive Group A cars for Mazda, but he was never again the force that he had been with Peugeot, though he later notched up more success in the desert.

Juha Kankkunen

The amazing Juha Kankkunen was at the top of World rallying, or thereabouts, for almost two decades – actually from 1983 to 2000. In that time, not only did he win 23 World rallies, but they spanned 1985 (the Safari – what a way to start!) to 1999 (Argentina), in a whole variety of cars. Even so, in all that time, he spent only one season – 1986 – with Peugeot – though in that one year he became World Rally Champion.

Although the tall and handsome young Finn seemed to love being on the golf course just as much as he enjoyed driving a rally car, he was by no means the same sort of rounded character as a Mikkola, or a Vatanen. Nor was he as effective on asphalt as on loose gravel or snow, and always expressed a dislike of asphalt challenges. Even so, if there was a regular, hard-grafting, rallying (as opposed to a PR) job to be done, employers from Peugeot to Ford, Toyota, Lancia, and Subaru were all ready to hire him.

Having started, way back, in a Ford Escort (didn't everyone?), he was drafted into the Toyota World Championship team, effectively as 'the apprentice' in 1983, to drive Celica Twin Cam Turbos, impressing everyone with his mature approach to the sport. Not only did he win two World events for Toyota in 1985 – Safari and Ivory Coast, no less, the two real marathons – but he attracted Jean Todt's attention, so much that he was rapidly signed up for 1986.

As the event-by-event story has made clear, not only did Juha then win the World Championship in 1986, but he won three individual rounds, with two second places. Once Peugeot withdrew from World rallying, Juha had to find work elsewhere, so in the next decade he drove for Lancia, Toyota, Lancia again, Toyota again, Ford, and Subaru, before ending his front-line career in 2001 when he was over 40 years of age. Like Carlos Sainz, even when he was not winning, he was often there and thereabouts at the end of events. Not only did he win no fewer than 23 World rallies (few have done better than this), but he also notched up 33 second places, and 19 third places, too – a remarkably consistent record in a long career.

Visit Veloce on the web – www.veloce.co.uk
Details of all books in print • Special offers • New book news • Gift vouchers

Competition story

When motorsport supremo Jean Todt called a press conference at the end of 1981, stating that Peugeot was to develop a four-wheel drive Group B car, he forecast that the first prototype would run in 1983, and that the new model would be homologated in 1984. He also stated, boldly, that the car would be good enough to win the Makes Championship in 1985.

Each and every one of those predictions came true, and if the FIA had not abruptly killed off the Group B rallying category in 1986, the 205 T16 would certainly have been winning World events in the 1987 and 1988 seasons, too.

1983

As we now know, the very first car ran on 16 February 1983, with French veteran Jean-Pierre Nicolas behind the wheel. At this time it was in fully-trimmed road car guise for rally development, and, in particular, the design of the first evolution machine had not then been completed. One of Todt's first priorities was to rationalise motorsport activities. First of all he abruptly closed down existing departments at Sochaux (near Mulhouse, the traditional HQ of Peugeot in eastern France), and at the Testing Centre at La Garenne. Then, after a brisk search for premises close to Paris, he discovered workshops at rue Paul Bert, not too far from the centre of the city. Not only did this keep Todt and his team close to the 'corridors of power' at Peugeot, it also meant that his department was conveniently close to many French writers and photographers who were concentrating on rallying.

Because the aim was originally to get homologated works cars on to the start line of the Monte Carlo Rally in January 1984 (that debut eventually slipped to the Tour de Corse in May 1984, for the car could not go rallying until the production run of 200 near-identical road cars – all of them painted in gun-metal grey, by the way – had been completed), much of 1983 was taken up by patient testing and development. Fortunately for Todt, Peugeot had extensive, modern, testing facilities at Mortfontaine, outside Paris – and, of course, there were thousands of miles of demanding roads in the Alps, close to the Mediterranean, where the authorities could be relied upon to turn a blind eye just so long as they knew it was a French team testing!

The original assessment period was fraught, to say the least, for the T16's structure was soon found to need strengthening (and weight was always the enemy), the engine's power output had to be improved (the engine had to be made reliable, too – which it not always was, at first), and the handling of what was a rear-heavy car had to be improved. Even at that point it was found that the rally car did not 'fly' very well over big jumps. Although this defect had to be shrugged off at first, as the car's overall performance increased over time it became more serious – this would be exemplified with near-fatal results to Ari Vatanen in Argentina in 1985.

After hopes of entry in the high-profile/high-publicity Mille Pistes event in high summer had been abandoned (the car was not considered rally-ready, and Todt was not willing for his team to be humiliated), the T16 was rarely seen in public, though testing continued. Then, at the end of October 1983, came the only occasion where it actually competed in an event before homologation was achieved.

This was the Trophee Francois Piot (Sarlat) Rally, which was held in the Dordogne at the end of October. The hard-working test car (chassis number P1) was re-furbished, made

From almost any angle, the 205 T16 was an elegant little hatchback – though this colour scheme was not normally applied to road cars.

Except that extra driving lamps and decals would eventually be added, the first-ever T16, unveiled in February 1983, was not visually changed before it was ready to go rallying.

to look extremely smart in Peugeot-Talbot Sport Colours, and entrusted to Jean-Pierre 'Jumbo' Nicolas for the day on what was a short event which rather lacked in publicity. [Ford would later use similar thinking with the Escort RS Cosworth in 1990, by entering it in a minor event in Spain, if it should fail on its first event, then that disaster would be shrugged off, but if it should succeed, all manner of praise would be heaped on it ...]

This was a credible, if not sensational, first outing. Even though it was running with the latest turbocharged 1.8-litre engine, which was producing 300bhp, Nicolas could only finish second overall – to a works Citroën Visa 1000 Pistes Group B car, a car, incidentally, which might have had four-wheel drive, but had only a 135bhp/1.4-litre engine. If nothing else, this confirmed that an effective four-wheel drive system – and the 1000 Pistes installation was certainly that – could make up for other deficiencies.

Accordingly, 'Jumbo' pronounced himself satisfied with the result (though he thought there was too much understeer – that was obvious to track-side observers) and Jean Todt made the expected upbeat remarks about the new car, though he must have been disappointed by the time that it was taking to get the new model into rallying. In some ways the T16 had worked well right 'out of the box', but a great deal of work was needed to make it ready to tackle Audi's Quattro in 1984.

1984

And that, for the next five months, was that. During the winter of 1983/84 Peugeot eventually built the 200 'homologation' T16 road cars in a special facility at its (ex-Chrysler-France) factory at Poissy, near Paris, lining them up theatrically for inspection (and for counting) by FISA, homologation being granted on 1 April 1984. The first evolution of 20 more specialised cars, which were lined up in the PTS department, were also approved at the same time. Those

On or off sealed surfaces, the 205 T16 had an extremely effective four-wheel drive chassis, even in road-car form.

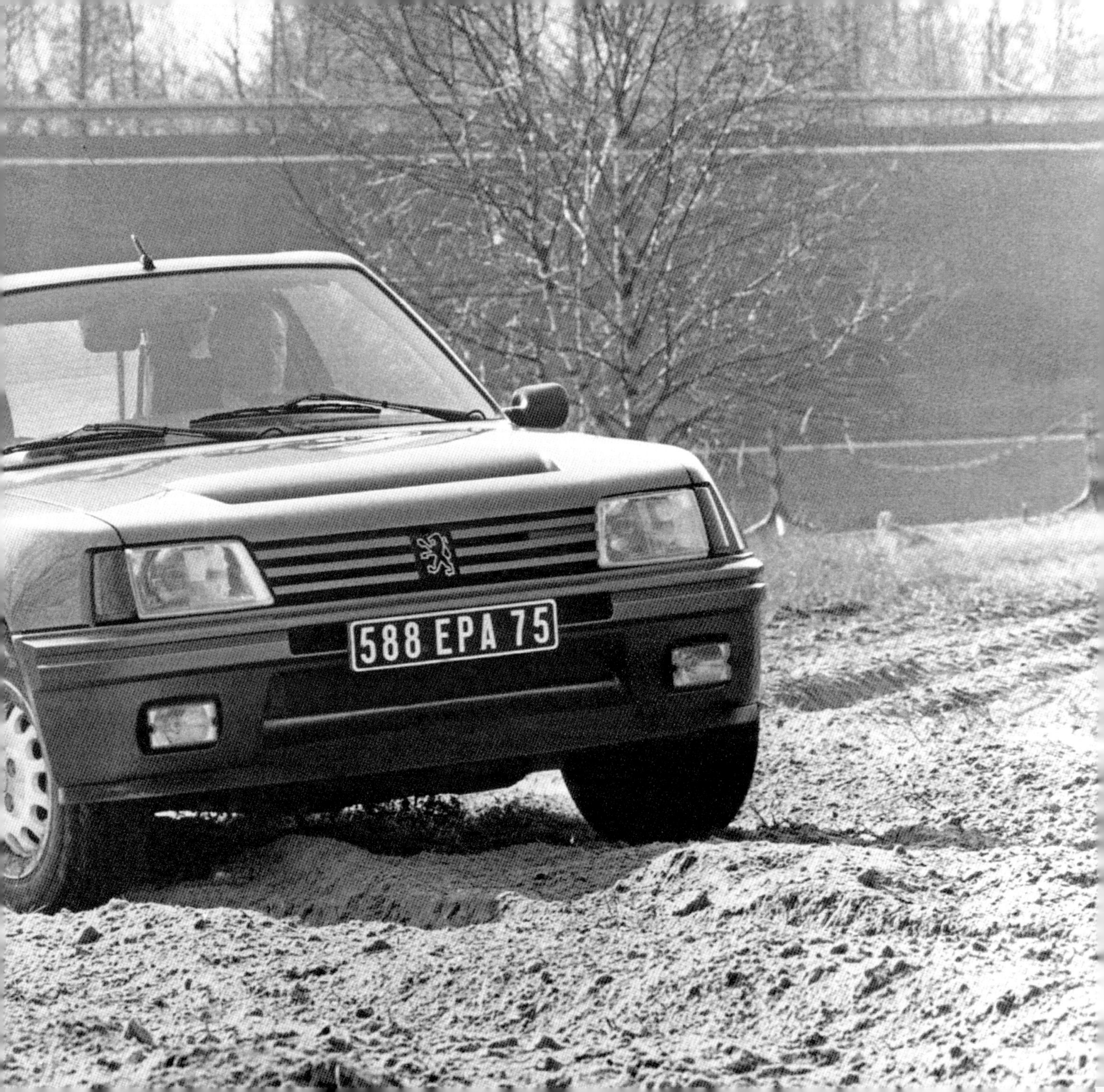
588 EPA 75

Although the 205 T16 was a fully-fledged 200-off Group B car, Peugeot made sure that road-going versions were very carefully and tastefully equipped. Because the engine and transmission were behind the seats, this was only a two-seater.

Rally car dashboards do not normally look as neat and tidy as this – but even as early as February 1983 Jean Todt's engineers had worked out where, and how, all the 205 T16's instrumentation should be placed.

Previous Peugeot rally cars

Until it decided to go ahead with the 205 T16 programme, Peugeot had never been completely dedicated to a serious rally programme, nor produced any 'homologation specials'. Originally, its solid family cars – particularly the 404 and 504 saloons and the V6-engined 504 Coupé – had proved their worth on events like the East African Safari, where structural strength rather than straight-line performance was all-important at the time.

Later, in the 1970s, the company came to concentrate on the 504 range – saloons and fixed-head coupés – particularly as these cars had more performance than the 404s, and also enjoyed all-independent suspension, which improved their traction in many off-highway situations. Victory in the 1975 East African Safari was a real triumph, and in 1978 this rugged performance was further emphasised when Peugeot used 2.7-litre V6-engined cars to win once again. However, because these cars could always be outpaced by more specialised competition cars, Peugeot was obliged to hire superstar drivers like Ove Andersson, Hannu Mikkola and Simo Lampinen to try to make up for that deficiency. One element of continuity was provided by the Frenchman Jean-Pierre 'Jumbo' Nicholas, who not only won the Safari for the 504 in 1978, but was an invaluable test/development driver for the 205 T16 in the 1980s.

All 200 205 T16s were left-hand drive and had a neatly equipped fascia like this. The drilled pedals were not only functional but made an artistic point, too.

were the twenty cars which PTS (and its associates, to which it could supply ready-made examples) would use in the first 18 months or so – quite enough for a full-blooded programme, with allowance for practice, testing, and maybe even a major accident or so!

Naturally (for its sub-title was 'Rally de France'), it was highly appropriate that the car's very first appearance in a World rally should be on the island of Corsica, in the Tour de Corse of May 1984, where PTS put in a big effort, even though it knew full well that its engines were still not as powerful as they might be – and would need to be. Not only did it have two brand new 335bhp cars – (chassis numbers C1 and C2) – but these were to be driven by

Peugeot produced all 200 205 T16 'homologation cars' by the end of March 1984, this being absolutely typical of the breed. Everything, including the air scoop ahead of the rear wheel, is totally functional.

By later standards, of course, the 205 T16 lacked aerodynamic 'add-on' spoilers and wings, but had an extremely well-balanced chassis.

Peugeot homologated the T16 on 1 April 1984, and entered two cars in the Tour de Corse just five weeks later. Driving this car, Ari Vatanen set no fewer than seven fastest stage times, and five second-fastests, before crashing the car on standing water in a stage, after which the poor car caught fire and was destroyed.

Ari Vatanen and Jean-Pierre Nicolas. It would have been better to have 360-400bhp, but this tune was simply not available at that time.

In a good fairy tale, of course, I would now be able to write that Ari Vatanen won the event on his first outing for Peugeot, but in fact the record books show that he crashed his car, and that it was the ever-reliable, ever-pragmatic, Jean-Pierre Nicolas who took fourth place. More, surely, could not have been expected – Peugeot had never before been running a competitive car which was likely to win, Ari Vatanen had joined the team after a rather lack-lustre season in Rothmans-sponsored Opels, while Nicolas had actually come out of retirement to get involved in the programme.

Even so, for a first outing it was a good, solid performance (far more satisfactory than its rivals could ever have feared), sending all the right signals to Peugeot management, and to the pundits. It left Todt's Peugeot team knowing that the chassis was already good, and confirmed that the still-new

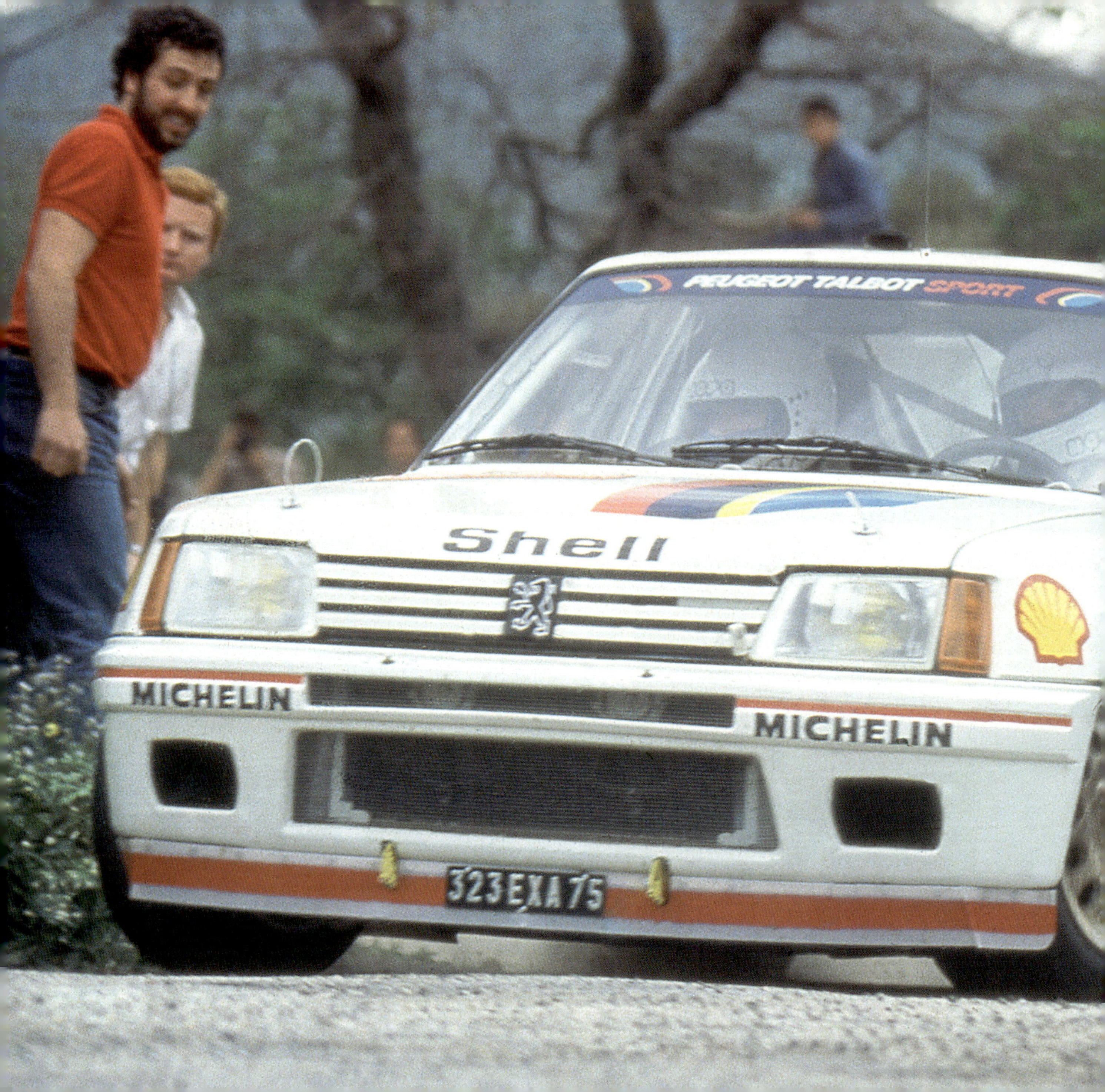
PEUGEOT TALBOT SPORT
Shell
MICHELIN
MICHELIN
323EXA75

engine had a power-deficiency (with only 320bhp/2.2 bar of boost at first, but 335bhp for Corsica, they had suspected this for some months). Further, they knew (because rallying's grapevine was as active as ever, and had told them so) that Lancia was already working on a new and very powerful 4WD Group B contender (this was the Delta S4, which would go rallying from late 1985), and that Ford's four-wheel drive mid-engined RS200 would also break cover before the end of the year. There was not a second to lose ...

Although the new Peugeots impressed everyone with their grace and agility, and eventually set ten fastest special stage times (of a total of 30 stages) on the serpentine tarmac roads of Corsica, they were not yet dominant. Attilio Bettega's rear-drive Lancia Rally 037 led for the first seven stages before hitting a roadside rock in fog and losing much time having repairs made, after which Vatanen led until half distance. Ari seemed to be going quicker and quicker as he got more used to the car, but eventually the car got away from him, and crashed out after his Michelins aquaplaned on a pool of standing water on the first stage of the final leg of the event. Although the car turned over, caught fire and eventually burnt out, neither Ari nor his co-driver Terry Harryman were hurt. Corsica is one of those especially demanding islands which makes no allowances for 100 per cent committed drivers who occasionally overstep the mark (which Ari certainly was): the records show that he was never to win an event on this island.

This mishap handed the lead to Markku Alen's Lancia Rally 037, and Jean-Pierre Nicolas finally ended up fourth (to quote Todt: 'There was only one thing to do. We had to carry Jean-Pierre to the finish, on our backs if necessary ...'). An indication of the resources that Peugeot was prepared to pump into this revitalised team is that JPN's car would never again be used on a rally, although in the team records it turns up a number more times as a practice/test machine.

Works T16s always looked immaculate until, that is, the drivers managed to nibble away at their spoilers and more vulnerable corners! This was Ari Vatanen on the car's very first appearance in homologated form – Tour de Corse 1984 – when it crashed and was destroyed by fire.

As a result of this outing, Peugeot realised that the 205 T16 still had serious development problems to be overcome, confirming that no amount of testing could substitute for actual competition. On this tarmac rally, which put such a heavy demand on the braking system, the team discovered that the disc rotors themselves were prone to overheating, and that the assemblies were tending to shake themselves apart. Additionally, even without the rigours of rough-road driving, suspension problems (due to inadequate damping) were already apparent, so much so that after the Acropolis the team turned to Bilstein of Germany for damper supplies – Bilstein's gas-filled products were seen as the best that could be fitted to modern rally cars.

Four weeks (and more frenzied testing) later, the team arrived in Greece to tackle the Acropolis with two more brand-new cars (chassis C3 and C4), facing up to an event which was then recognised as the roughest, toughest, dustiest and hottest in the World Championship calendar. Because this would be the very first time that the T16 had competed on a truly rough-road event, Todt was not really expecting a victory, but was certainly praying for a competitive showing. No-one, however, seems to have relayed Todt's forebodings to the remarkable Ari Vatanen (who had already won the Acropolis in 1980 and 1981, both times in Ford Escorts), for he led the event, briefly, at one period, and set no fewer than eleven fastest stage times (of 37 stages), with ten other 'podium' times to back up the demonstration of PTS engineering. Only Stig Blomqvist, in an Audi Quattro, recorded more truly fast times than that.

After this event it was Martin Holmes, in his prestigious annual book *World Rallying 7*, who summed up the impact

Peugeot 16-valve engines

The founding fathers of the 205 T16 were lucky in that, at exactly the time they were starting to engineer the new rally car, high-performance versions of Peugeot's modern XU engine family were also on the way.

The first of the XU family, a 1580cc engine with a single overhead camshaft cylinder head and two valves per cylinder, was introduced in the autumn of 1982, fitted immediately to the new Citroën BX family car, and within months was added to the Peugeot 305, and to other models in the Peugeot-Citroën range. At that point the 1580cc engine had an 83mm bore and a 73mm stroke.

At that time, though, there were still no enlarged types, nor twin-overhead-camshaft cylinder head derivatives immediately ready. However, by the mid-1980s, a 1905cc engine had arrived (with a stroke of 88mm), so it is easy to see why the 205 T16 design team opted to use a 1775cc version (with a stroke of 82mm), for this could be comfortably accommodated within the existing (strengthened) light-alloy cylinder block. As explained in the main text, the use of this odd engine capacity was imposed on the engineers because, when turbocharged it was deemed to be a 2.5-litre power unit ...

In later years, Peugeot produced 16-valve versions of this road-car engine, but the cylinder head layout was vastly different from that originally engineered for the 205 T16.

Main picture: Jean-Pierre Nicolas, committed as usual, pushing an early T16 to its limits on the 1984 Acropolis Rally.

Right: Ari Vatanen on the 1984 Acropolis Rally, the team's second outing with the T16. He set many fastest times before the engine failed, something which was a rarity on this model.

Far right: Throughout 1984, chief test driver Jean-Pierre Nicolas was a worthy second-string works driver behind mega-star Ari Vatanen. Here he is seen in the early stages of the 1984 Acropolis – before the ultra-rough roads caused suspension trouble, and forced his withdrawal.

PEUGEOT TALBOT SPORT
ROTHMANS
31 ACROPOLIS RALLY
12
Shell
MICHELIN
Valeo
speedline

3

Rothmans
12
MICHELIN

of these new cars so perfectly: 'The 205 Turbo 16s had proved so good on the asphalt roads of Corsica, conditions that were not so immediately advantageous, that on the gravel tracks in Greece it was expected they would murder the opposition, while they lasted. The cars looked so right. They seemed to float over the rough parts, the drivers could turn the car into corners in rear-wheel drive slides, they had none of the brute force which the heavy, big Quattros demanded.'

Unhappily, at this stage in their development they were still not quite strong enough to make it through to the finish. Vatanen eventually took the lead after 17 stages when the Audis were wilting in the heat, but a double engine failure in his T16 – first a broken fuel pump drive belt, then a blown turbocharger – pegged him back, and problems later recurred even after repairs had been made. Winning at this level, it seemed, wasn't going to be easy – but the experienced Vatanen/Todt/Nicolas axis knew this very well, and they also realised that the failures being experienced could be solved by upgrading the specifications. The good news, surely, was that the structure had stood up well to the rough roads in Greece, for until and unless the team tackled the Safari there would be no more structural demand on the car than here.

To Peugeot's joy, the first victory then followed in Finland (the 1000 Lakes) in August, where Vatanen, a real folk hero if ever there was one, would win his domestic rally. Todt wisely excused the Frenchman, Jean-Pierre Nicolas, from taking part in the 'Finnish Grand Prix', which made very specific demands on the drivers. Instead he elected to send Ari all on his own, in yet another brand-new car (C5). This was the first to use the improved engine (development work was proceeding all the time), which was now rated at 350bhp, with 2.5 bar of boost. Ari spent weeks practicing for the event, and it was thought that the new Peugeots would be ideal for the fast, sweeping (though loose-surfaced) stages of rural Finland.

Ari, of course, was quite determined to win his 'local' event (he had last succeeded with a Rothmans-sponsored Ford Escort RS in 1981 – Ford had not won a World event

Early in the 1000 Lakes of 1984, Ari Vatanen's car was looking immaculate, and already leading the event ...

... but towards the end there was minor damage around the lower centre of the front spoiler. Nothing, really, by Vatanen standards!

since then), and stamped his authority all over it by setting 31 fastest stage times, 12 second fastests and four third fastests in a 50 stage event – a crushing demonstration. Victory was all the more sweet because along the way he defeated several other Scandinavian superstars, including Stig Blomqvist (Quattro), Markku Alen (Lancia Rally 037) and Henri Toivonen (Lancia Rally 037).

If we agree that the Audi Quattro was no more than an energetically produced and developed conversion of a front-wheel drive coupé, this 1000 Lakes success was, incidentally, the first-ever World victory by a purpose-built four-wheel drive rally car. Although we didn't know it at the time, this was a real turning point in the history of World rallying.

Not that it was as easy to win as Peugeot finally made it seem, for, in the run up to the event, the team had discovered to their dismay that the practice cars were not handling well over the many high-speed jumps. This was an early and ominous indication that in certain conditions and at certain speeds, the T16 was likely to land nose-down after a jump, which often gave the driver a hard time. After a long, fast, high jump (and there were many of those in Finland!) the car would feel, and look, most unstable until the brave Vatanen wrestled it back into shape.

Pre-event development of damper settings, spring rates and ride heights all helped in detail (though at one stage, overnight panic deliveries from Bilstein in Germany were needed), but even Ari admitted that he felt uneasy at times. Ari, being Ari, coped well – where other drivers certainly could not.

The world, of course, already knew just how good the blond Finnish hero was, and now it suddenly realised that Jean Todt and his engineers had finally got their technical sums right with the 205 T16 as well. With just this one entry to run against the works might of Lancia, Audi, Toyota and Nissan, and to beat them all, fair and square, had made their point. To its eternal credit, Peugeot had never boasted, up-front, that it was going to change the face of rallying – it just set out to do that, ready to celebrate if plans turned into achievements – which they duly did. It took only three events to start winning, and they had been competitive from the moment that the first car started the first stage in Corsica.

Accordingly, please remember that first victory – 1000 Lakes 1984 – and the Paris registration number of the works T16 – 704 EXC 75 – which Vatanen was driving, and mark them down as pivotal in rally history. The rallying world

A famous victory – Ari Vatanen and Terry Harryman drove serenely to win the Rally of 1000 Lakes in August 1984. It was the first of many successes for this combination.

changed from that day, Sunday, 28 August 1984. Forget all about Audi and the battleship engineering of its massive five-cylinder machines – this was the true birth of the high-tech Group B era.

Four weeks later (and yet more hard grinding of testing, practice, and the building of more new cars), two new machines – C6 and C7 in the PTS chassis number sequence – were made ready for two drivers to take the start of the San Remo Rally in Italy. Here, of all places, Peugeot's biggest rival, Lancia, was determined to put up a good performance on its home event (the nationalistic Italian press had made it clear that victory was expected), but Lancia still used the obsolescent rear-drive Rally 037s. It was going to be a long event (54 stages), spread over six days, and there would be many kilometres of tarmac and rough-road surfaces.

As it happened, San Remo was almost a complete

walkover for Peugeot, as a bald statement of results makes clear. Out of 54 stages, many of which were on gravel surfaces, Ari Vatanen set no fewer than 31 fastest times, and nine second fastests: eventually he won the event by no less than 5min 27sec. No matter that a formidable team of four Lancia Rally 037s disputed his right to win in their own country: Ari knew better than that.

Nothing that Lancia or Audi (whose works cars were short-wheelbase Sport models on this event) could do was a match for this, and not even a minor 'Ari accident' at one point, when his car spun helplessly on standing water (which wiped off the driving lamps, but did little other damage), could stop him.

If the 205 T16 had fundamental remaining faults at this stage of its career, they were that it was still a little too heavy and needed more power to match the Audi Quattros, whose Sport model was now using 450bhp, apparently with engine reliability but with very difficult handling characteristics. Even so, seasoned veteran Jean-Pierre Nicolas could not extract the same performance as his more illustrious team-mate (he only recorded a single third fastest on a stage, nothing higher than that, and could only take fifth place), and it was becoming clear that he would not be driving for the team again in 1985.

Ari saved his most spectacular drive of the season until November, when his was the only 205 T16 Peugeot sent to start Britain's RAC Rally. This was the same car with which he had won the San Remo event – in fact it was the first works car to start two events. Although Ari was a hero to many thousands of British rally fans (they had fallen in love with his skills and charisma during his seven years in Ford Escorts) what actually unfolded during this marathon 56 special stage event could not possibly have been better scripted by a Hollywood wordsmith. After taking a very big lead on the first four days, Ari then rolled his car and lost the lead. Nothing daunted, he then took it back to Peugeot service, saw it speedily repaired, only to have it break a driveshaft at the start of the Dovey complex. Once again the lead was lost, and he only regained it five stages from the end!

As Todt later commented Ari: "... spun out of control due to fatigue or carelessness. He tumbled off the road in a somersault ..."

Fortunately, bodyshell damage was slight, so after a

This San Remo 1984 study shows how Peugeot mechanics gained easy access to the mid-mounted engine/transmission of the 205 T16.

Right: Throughout 1984 Jean-Pierre Nicolas was Peugeot's anchor-man, carrying out all the team's testing and development, and backing up Ari Vatanen on his dashes for victory. This was San Remo in 1984, where he took fifth place.

Ari Vatanen and Terry Harryman won the 1984 San Remo Rally, humiliating the Lancia team along the way ...

... and never lacked for commitment. Co-driver Terry Harryman prefers not to watch!

In spite of rolling their car at one stage, and breaking the transmission at another, Ari Vatanen and Terry Harryman won the 1984 RAC Rally in fine style.

Right: Spectator control on the 1984 San Remo Rally was flimsy, to say the least – but Jean-Pierre Nicolas was too busy to take much notice of that.

change of windscreen everything appeared normal again. And when the time came to replace the transmission following driveshaft failure, the mechanics changed a complete back axle and centre differential in nine minutes – a time of which Vatanen's old Escort colleagues at Boreham (including the formidable Mick Jones) would have been proud!

Not that the serene Finn ever seemed to be downcast. Of 56 stages, he set 33 fastest times, and 13 second fastests, with only Hannu Mikkola in the old-type long-wheelbase Audi Quattro even able to stay on terms and finishing in second place, having led that part of the event where Ari was experiencing his dramas.

Quite suddenly, it seemed, the still-developing Peugeot team had become standard-setters, and on any loose-surface event it had become the team to beat. Having recorded three victories in consecutive entries (in very different conditions, each time), and with what looked like consummate ease, the 205 T16 had suddenly made all existing Group B cars look obsolete. Although PTS was already working hard to develop the Second evolution derivative of the car, Jean Todt and his technical chief, Andre de Cortanze, thought there were more victories to follow. They were right.

As *Autosport's* Rallies Editor, Peter Foubister, commented in his annual, end-of-season review of 1984: "Peugeot led the way, headed

79

By winning the 1984 RAC Rally, Ari Vatanen and Terry Harryman made it three victories in successive events for the 205 T16. If we are to believe registration numbers, this car – 128 FBL 75 – had already won the San Remo Rally a few weeks earlier.

Peugeot T16 drivers needed to see exactly where they were going, which explains the battery of six extra driving lamps for a night-time session – all of which could be speedily removed by the service crews when daylight returned.

every event that they entered, and finished a short campaign with a string of successes. Suddenly, Ari Vatanen lost his life-at-the-limit reputation, swapping it for the cool, calculating, professional approach and underlying the potential of the Turbo 16.

"While [Jean] Todt's engineers have obviously excelled in the design of the 205, and Todt has worked tirelessly to gain the absolute confidence of the whole company (and hence a total financial commitment to the project), it is the construction of his team in such a short space of time that is perhaps the greatest achievement. Certainly, shortcuts have been taken with key people in the right jobs, but the bulk of the mechanics involved were newcomers and many had not even seen a rally stage before they signed on ..."

1985

Before the new season started in Monte Carlo in January, PTS completely re-jigged its driving strength, and braced itself to tackle all events, anywhere, in whatever conditions were thrown at it. As expected, Ari Vatanen stayed on as the undisputed team leader, while Jean-Pierre Nicolas finally retired, to take up a new PTS post as head of the Sport Promotion Department. Even so, it was typical of the ambitious Todt (and the backing he enjoyed from his bosses) that to take his place, he did not hire just one new driver – but two! Even so, they say that at this point he had to convince his bosses that at that time there were no French rally drivers who could match Ari Vatanen's talents (nor, as it happens, would there ever be one ...).

80

Not that Todt managed to carry out his initial masterplan – for he tried hard to sign up the German double World Champion Walter Rohrl (from Audi), but failed, and also tried to attract another flamboyant Finn, Markku Alen (from Lancia), and failed again. Not everyone, it seemed, wanted to take up what Todt assured them would be 'equal number one' status in a team where their partner would be Ari Vatanen! To expect this of a team whose lead driver had already won eight World events (and the last three had been for Peugeot) stretched credibility too far.

Todt then turned his attention to two other Finnish personalities – Henri Toivonen (who was with Lancia), and Timo Salonen (Nissan) – and finally settled on Salonen. Up to this time, incidentally, Timo had never rallied a four-wheel drive car before he signed up with Peugeot.

Finally, for a third driver, an 'apprentice' almost, he

The T16 didn't seem to mind whether it was asked to tackle tarmac, loose surfaces, ice and snow – or water! This was a deep water splash in an early event in 1984.

Perfect Christmas card setting, maybe, but treacherous driving conditions – Monte Carlo 1985, with Ari Vatanen on his way to a famous victory.

signed up a young Frenchman, Bruno Saby, hoping that he could develop his talents and reap rewards (and much chauvinistic publicity) in the future.

The programme lined up at the start of the year was so vast that it would have looked daunting to any team manager,

Bruno Saby was signed by Peugeot as its third driver for 1985, with only a limited programme in prospect, but following Ari Vatanen's huge accident in Argentina he was rapidly promoted to full-time status.

but by this time the team had so much success behind it, and such a build-up of experience, that it was convinced that it could cope. It thought that the car was now capable of winning anywhere, at any time – and so it could. Peugeot planned to start no fewer than eleven World rallies – sometimes with three cars – and in the end would win six of these, and would easily win the World Rally Championship for Makes.

Three cars were ready for Monte Carlo – two of them being brand new, the third being 'C6' for Bruno Saby, which was the ex-Nicolas car from San Remo. Because this was a winter rally, naturally everyone expected much snow, but, in fact, many of the stages were on part clear, part old ice and snow, which made conditions very difficult for everyone, especially for the 'ice notes' crews advising the drivers on which tyres to choose for each stage.

Even though Ari slid off in the snow on an early stage and up-ended some spectators (fortunately there were no injuries, though pictures of the accidents were horrifying), everything started well for the team, and Ari was comfortably leading until suddenly (and for no good reason that he could ever explain afterwards), Ari's co-driver, Terry Harryman of Northern Ireland, checked him in four minutes early at a time control (there had been delays earlier on, and a misunderstanding about a revised schedule): this, according to the draconian rules being applied by the Monegasques (even to French crews, who usually got the benefit of any doubt that was going), meant that Ari therefore suffered a penalty of eight minutes.

Was victory therefore lost? Not according to the uncannily-talented Vatanen, for he clawed everything back with incredible determination, benefited from mistakes made by his rivals in tyre choice, and finally regained the lead seven stages from the end. He finally won by a magisterial five minutes (or by thirteen 'stage' minutes, which was quite incredible in the circumstances).

No fewer than 21 of the 33 stages fell to Ari, who was second or third fastest on another ten stages. Timo Salonen, still learning his 4x4 craft, finished third for Peugeot, with Bruno Saby fifth. Peugeot dominance after not winning a Monte Carlo Rally for 53 years? You could say that ...

Just two weeks later, Peugeot pitched up in Sweden, where Ari and Timo used the self-same cars they had driven so serenely in Monte Carlo: not only did that prove just how solidly-built the latest T16s actually were, but what an easy time, structurally and technically, these two machines had had in Monte Carlo.

Since both the drivers were Scandinavians, rallying in conditions which had been second nature to them from the first day they ever slid behind the wheel of a car, and since the 205 T16s handled demonstrably better than any other car in rallying, it seemed that victory was assured – if the cars did not break down.

Here's a novelty – dry roads, but snow on the sides, in a very sunny section of the 1985 Monte Carlo Rally. Even though co-driver Terry Harryman made a time-keeping error which could have been serious, Ari was much the fastest of all drivers in the event, the team eventually winning by more than five minutes.

83

Just – and only just – in control, this T16 is perilously close to one of the ever-present snow banks in the Swedish rally of 1985. Ari Vatanen's car, carrying competition number 2, would win the event, with new team member Timo Salonen third in number 6.

The cars survived, and victory – the fifth consecutive win for the T16 in five World starts – was duly delivered. Once again it was Ari Vatanen who won, once again Timo Salonen was third, and once again it was works teams such as Audi which were found to be floundering. Without acknowledged winter-rallying heroes like Hannu Mikkola and Stig Blomqvist behind the wheel of the Audis, they could now offer no contest to the fleet and agile Peugeots. The T16s, incidentally, now had more power than ever before, though they were still not on a par with the brutally powerful Audis – and, in any case, the big advances in specification were being held back for the second evolution car, whose homologation was not expected until 1 April.

Then, in Portugal, the pattern was broken – although Peugeot won the event (I almost wrote 'as usual', for the pundits were beginning to expect it!), it was not Ari Vatanen behind the wheel! On only his third works drive for the team, it was Timo Salonen who delivered, though this time it was consistency rather than pace which defeated Walter Rohrl in the short-wheelbase Quattro. Not even a broken steering rack could sideline him.

And Ari? Surprisingly, he never led the rally at any stage, for Salonen seemed to be his equal on the asphalt stages. Later, what looked like a harmless rear puncture caused damage to the suspension, which subsequently collapsed. Perhaps his hard-working car (C11 – which had won the two previous events) was finally protesting after competing three times in two months!

Then came the East African Safari, where PTS was finally brought down to earth with a bump. This was to be expected really, for no team tends to go to East Africa, and get it right first time. It was not that Peugeot had never won the Safari before – quite the contrary, for Ove Andersson had won in a 504 in 1975, and 'Jumbo' (Nicolas) in a 504 Coupé V6 in 1978. This, on the other hand, was the first time the 205 T16 had ever attempted to overcome the heat, the awful roads, and the dust of East Africa. With this in mind, the engines were slightly de-tuned, the bodyshells of three cars (two of them brand new) were much stiffened, and the gearing was adjusted.

Almost all of this work, and some assiduous testing and pre-event practice, seemed to be wasted when Vatanen's car began to suffer suspension trouble, and finally retired when a water-cooling radiator sprung a leak (this eventually caused engine failure), while Saby's car (which was that used by Salonen to win in Portugal) broke its chassis.

Salonen, used to the bomb-proof African performance of his previous Nissans (which were slow by comparison, but always carefully prepared), somehow kept going with a battered car which suffered any number of problems. In the end he took seventh place, though he was no fewer than 3 hours 51 minutes behind the winning Toyota Celica Twin-Cam Turbo, and was really the last of the European Supercar drivers to make it to the end.

Early days in 1984, when a works T16 shows off the way in which it used to kick up its tail in high speed jumps. The be-winged E2 would go a long way towards curbing that habit.

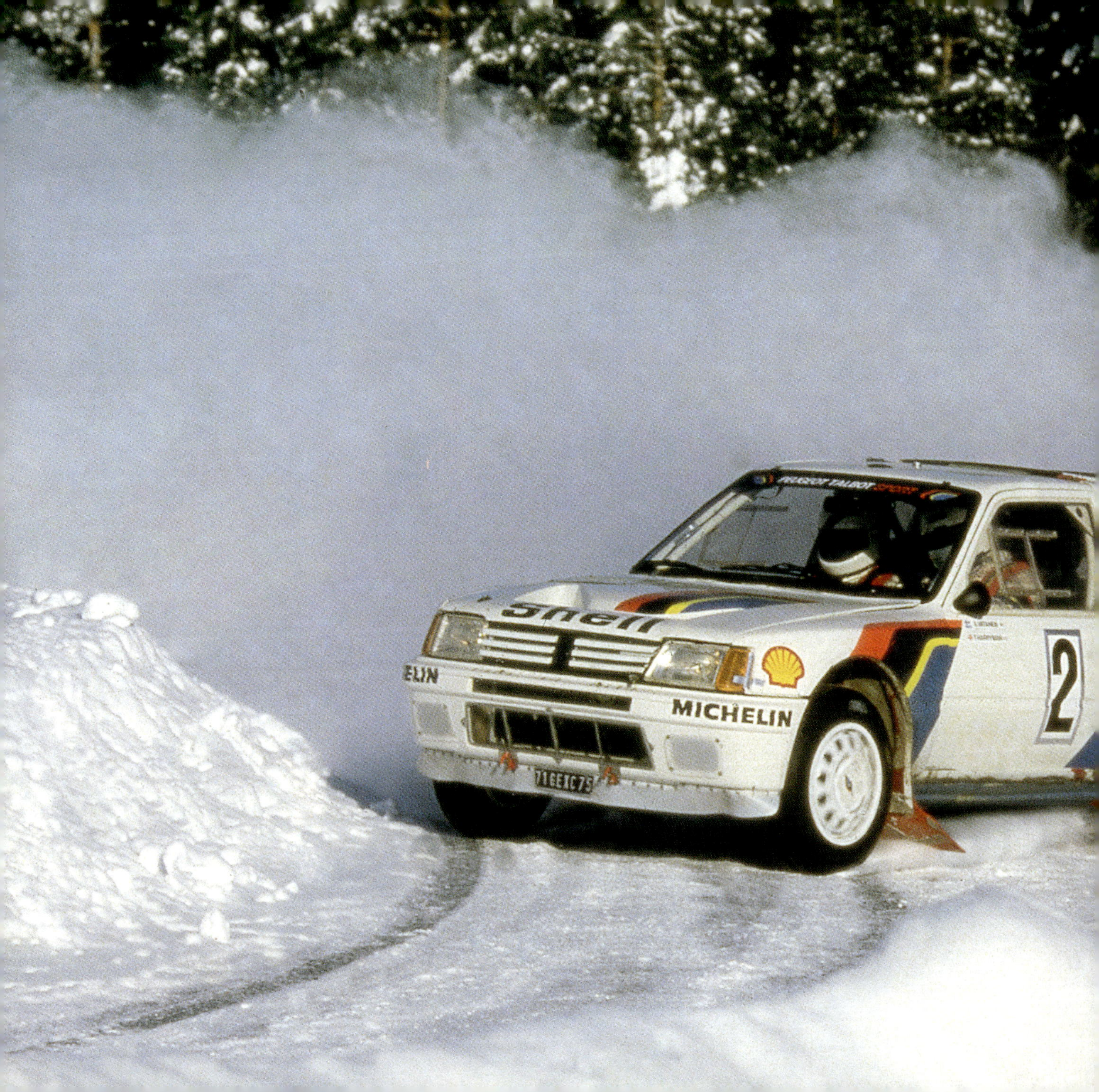
Shell
ELIN
MICHELIN
2

This was the sort of rabid popularity which the Group B generation of rally cars generated in the mid-1980s, with very little crowd control, especially in the 'Latin' countries. Although Peugeot's T16 was not involved in any grisly accidents, Jean Todt's organisation was always wary.

The T16's chassis was so well-developed that its top drivers could hurl it sideways through extraordinarily tight corners, and control would be maintained. This is Ari Vatanen on the way to an emphatic victory in Sweden, 1985.

For the 1985 Safari, Peugeot prepared three 'heavyweight' T16s to cope with the extra-tough conditions – the specifications including carrying a second spare wheel on the roof. But miracles take time in East Africa, only one car finished: Timo Salonen in seventh place.

Timo Salonen won his first World Rally championship event for Peugeot in Portugal in 1985, defeating every other works car by a country mile.

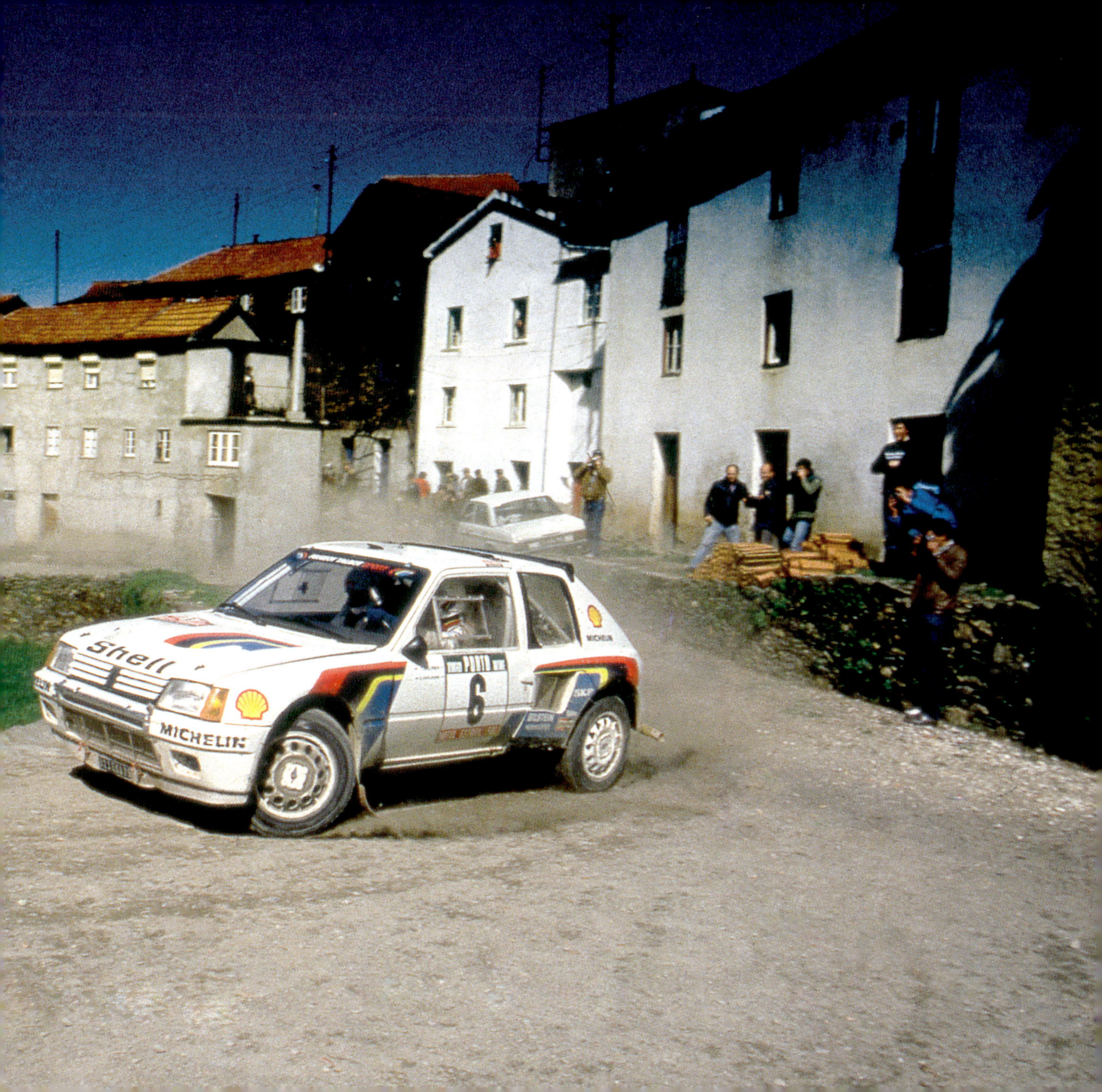
Shell
MICHELIN
PORTO
6

Although Ari Vatanen was always competitive, on the 1985 Safari in this very special 'heavyweight' T16, he eventually had to retire with head gasket failure.

Top: A battery of yellow-tinted lights, with snow on the tracks, identifies this as Ari Vatanen on his way to winning the 1985 Monte Carlo (Terry Harryman was his co-driver).

Above: When the time came to homologate the 'Evolution 2' derivative of the 205 T16 in April 1984, Peugeot went to enormous lengths to disguise the use of a big rear roof-top spoiler on the press photograph. If you look carefully, you will see that it is, indeed, there – but no other camera angle would have been so carefully chosen!

Jean Todt put a brave face on this, as well he might: "We were in the Safari to train for 1986," he later wrote. "We had a car which finished on our first attempt, there was nothing to be ashamed of ..."

Evolution 2 time

In the meantime, de Cortanze and his technical colleagues had been spending many months, and many midnight hours, working away on the next evolution of the T16, which I have already described on page 36, and for which twenty new cars had to be built. Even though the new model was homologated on 1 April – just a year after the original 205 T16 had been approved, in fact as early as the regulations allowed – the ever-pragmatic Todt was in no rush to commit it to the World Championship scene. After all, his original car was still only a year old, had been a consistent winner since the summer of 1984, and was by no means obsolete. As we now know, there was only a single E2 entry in the Tour de Corse, in April, then nothing until the 1000 Lakes in August.

Although it was Jean Ragnotti's rear-drive Renault Maxi 5 Turbo which completely dominated in Corsica, it was Peugeot's third driver, Bruno Saby, who took second place in the Evo 2 model. Although Bruno set only two fastest times, he was there and thereabouts throughout the event, which is just what Jean Todt had always hoped. Ari Vatanen, on the otherhand was faster, more often, in a 'new-old' car, but he suffered a double puncture on a very early stage, then set ten fastest times, before writing off his car in a high-speed crash (he had crashed in 1984, too, the T16's debut in World rallying). Timo Salonen's rally was even shorter-lived and more frustrating – for it suffered an engine failure even before it could complete a stage.

If this was not quite humiliation, it was a salutary lesson. The Peugeot team, therefore, returned to its base in Paris, licked its wounds, prepared two original-spec 'heavyweights'

Renault's mid-engined/rear-drive 5 Turbo was such an effective rally car that it must have tempted Peugeot to build the same sort of machine. Good enough to win the 1981 Monte Carlo Rally, it was soon swamped by the Audi Quattro, and the layout quickly consigned to the 'obsolete' bin.

(Vatanen's being brand-new, Salonen's being the car which had let him down in Corsica) – and immediately recovered its reputation in the Acropolis. Although Ari's car broke its steering on the second stage, Timo Salonen led from start to finish, setting nineteen fastest times and 26 second fastest times along the way. Not even Stig Blomqvist, in the fastest of the Audi Sport Quattros, could keep up, though he set more fastest times. It was Peugeot's first-ever success in the Acropolis, and to the tightly-knit circle of serious teams, this immediately elevated Peugeot to the 'top table'. Todt's conviction, that his car was really good enough to win anywhere, was being proved.

Four weeks later, for New Zealand, two more brand new old-type 205 T16s arrived, there appeared to be no

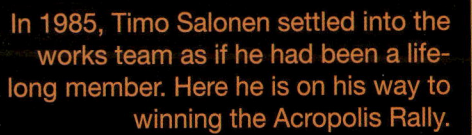

In 1985, Timo Salonen settled into the works team as if he had been a life-long member. Here he is on his way to winning the Acropolis Rally.

In the 1985 Tour de Corse Rally, T16 number 5 was driven to victory by Bruno Saby; behind him number 10 was driven by Michele Mouton. There doesn't seem to be any hurry to get the cars serviced ...

team orders, and after a spirited battle between Peugeot and Audi this proved to be yet another success for the French. Timo Salonen won the event, with Ari second to him, just 75 seconds behind after 46 stages and, if the truth be told, not satisfied with the outcome as this was an event he was yet to win). Clearly the two Peugeot drivers were very equally matched in New Zealand, and set virtually the same number of fast times; Peugeot was happy to record a 1-2 on this Asia-Pacific classic.

Then came Argentina, the high-speed rally which would make headlines in 1985 for all the wrong reasons. For Peugeot and the T16, some of the news was startlingly great – of the three cars which were sent (the ex-New Zealand cars and a third machine, ex-Acropolis, for former F1 star driver Carlos Reutemann), Timo Salonen won the event, with Reutemann third – but on the second stage Ari Vatanen's car crashed at high speed, getting written off in a roll and severely injuring both Ari and co-driver Terry Harryman. Although Terry made a remarkable recovery, Ari's life hung precariously in the balance for some weeks, and it was a long time before he again set foot in a rally car.

The Peugeot team, naturally, were totally distraught by this, especially as it became clear that the accident had followed a very high-speed end-over-end roll (of the sort always feared from this tail-heavy car). The good news – if any of it could be called good – was that although the car was totally written off, the structure of the car (and particularly the cabin, and the comprehensive roll cage) had stood up remarkably well to the multiple impact, for the cockpit layout was relatively little distorted. In the fullness of time, of course, Ari would make a complete recovery, and would go on to record further glories with the 'Grand Raid' version of this car, especially in Paris-Dakar rounds.

The only upbeat news which could be gleaned from this event was that it brought the original-type 205 T16's

The T16's four-wheel drive system was beautifully balanced, and extremely capable, on all types of going. In spite of the multitude of scoops and slats in the rear, the engines rarely suffered from dirt contamination.

PEUGEOT TALBOT SPORT
Shell
MICHELIN
MICHELIN
aerospatiale
25 FGV 75

Ex-F1 driver Carlos Reutemann drove the T16 only once, but finished a storming third in the rally of Argentina in 1985.

works career to a close – a career in which the cars had started 13 events (superstitious, anyone?), and won on nine of them, which was a quite remarkable result for a car which had been built with no previous appropriate engineering experience, no precedent, nor any technical heritage.

Even so, it was a sombre Peugeot team arriving in Finland only three weeks later. Two new cars were made ready for (de facto) team leader Timo Salonen, and for Kalle Grundel (who had been driving a 205 T16 with much success in German events), both of them more powerful E2 types, complete with extrovert spoilers (which, some thought, might have helped Vatanen's 'flight' in Argentina). In an event bitterly fought with the short-wheelbase Audi Sport Quattro E2s, the last of the rear-drive Lancia Rally 037s, and the rear-drive Toyota Celica Twin Cam Turbos, this proved to be a real Finnish GP. Although Blomqvist's

Audi Sport Quattro E2 was fast, Salonen's new-type Peugeot was faster, for in the end he won the event – it was his fifth of the season, and his fourth consecutive victory in this particular 205 T16 – by just 48 seconds: Grundel, not as fast, but very consistent, took fifth place.

Perhaps it was now asking too much of Lady Luck to provide Salonen (and Peugeot) with yet more victories in 1985 – and the pessimists were not disappointed. As it happened, the 1000 Lakes was not only Timo's last win of the season, but also that of the 205 T16 in 1985. But, why worry? By that time the team had secured the Makes and the Drivers' Championships, and was already planning ahead for 1986. Ari Vatanen, it was clear, would not be fit enough to start that season with it, but the 205 T16 E2 was looking better and stronger even than hoped.

In the last events of the season, therefore, Salonen took second in the Italian San Remo Rally (to Walter Rohrl's Audi Sport Quattro), while both cars were forced out of the ultra-long and gruelling RAC Rally of Great Britain (63 stages totalling 547 miles!). The RAC, in any case, was one where all the hype was concentrated on the first appearance of Austin-Rover's new four-wheel drive MG Metro 6R4, and on Lancia's new Delta S4, while Peugeot's Jean Todt spent much of his time whinging about the event's secret-stage format, which he said favoured British drivers. With two of his three drivers (Michael Sundstrom was in the third E1 type) off the road in accidents, and with Salonen out with an engine failure, maybe he had a point.

The news of Ari Vatanen's steady, but very gradual, recovery from his accident, continued to be good, which was a relief for every rally enthusiast in the world. Apart from the sombre memories of the reasons behind the accident, for Peugeot it had been an extremely successful year. In an intensive programme, the team had started all eleven rallies which counted for World Makes points, taking seven victories and two second places. No-one, surely, could expect it to match that record in 1986?

1986

Because Ari Vatanen was taking so long to recover from his awful accident in Argentina in 1985, for the new season Jean Todt had to look round for another front-line driver to take his place, as he was not sure that Kalle Grundel was quite what he wanted. Grundel left to drive the RS200 for Ford. Having re-signed Timo Salonen and Bruno Saby for 1986, he then captured the 26-year-old Finn, Juha Kankkunen, who had spent the previous two seasons learning his craft with Toyota (and with co-driver Fred Gallagher, which was an invaluable aid to progress).

Juha was not only looking forward to piloting a top-rank four-wheel drive rally car for the first time, but he linked up with a new co-driver, Juha Piironen. This signing proved to be quite inspired for Peugeot, for in an eleven-event season, Juha would win three times, finish second twice and third once. After a nail-biting finish to the season, where the outcome would depend on the status of the San Remo Rally (as we will see, it took weeks to settle this), Peugeot would also win the World Makes Championship for the second season. It was a season, however, quite overshadowed by personal disasters in rallying, which no-one recalls with any pleasure. If Todt and Peugeot had only known it in January,

Finland in 1985, with Timo Salonen on his way to recording Peugeot's second victory in the fast Finnish 1000 Lakes event.

this was the start of the 205 T16's third and final season in rallying.

The very first event of the year – Monte Carlo – showed that 1986 was going to witness a bitter battle between the Peugeots, and Lancia's newly-homologated Delta S4, cars which were of similar size and performance, but very different in their mechanical layout. Later in the season other cars, such as the MG Metro 6R4 and the Ford RS200, would figure on the sidelines, but would never affect the overall result.

In Monte Carlo, Henri Toivonen's Lancia beat Timo Salonen's Peugeot by a very comfortable four minutes, and analysis of the special stage times showed that on this occasion the Lancia was comfortably quicker than the T16. Toivonen, who had won the 1985 RAC Rally on the Lancia's first outing, looked quite inspired (though a little wild at the time). If we had only realised that this was to bring tragic consequences later in the season ...

Group B, it seemed, was now approaching its full majesty, for the results were dominated by Peugeot, Lancia, and Audi, and it was known that Ford (with its RS200) would join in at the next World round in Sweden. Four-wheel drive and more than 400bhp (both of which the T16 E2 had, and well-developed, too) were essential for any and all events. Even so, after the excitement of 1985, for Peugeot to finish second, fifth and sixth (the latter cars being a long way off the pace) was no more than an average result.

Fortunately, Peugeot's fortunes were turned around in Sweden where Juha Kankkunen recorded his first Peugeot victory by two minutes from Markku Alen's Lancia Delta S4, though Salonen's car had to retire after his engine lost all its oil. Kankkunen and Alen appeared to be equally matched- man against man, car against car – this was to be the recurring pattern throughout the 1986 season.

Juha Kankkunen was the 'find' of the 1986 season, the only one in which he competed for Peugeot, but in which he won the World Rally Championship. He picked up victories for Peugeot in Sweden, Greece and New Zealand, every time in an E2.

PEUGEOT
PEUGEOT TALBOT SPORT
Shell
4
MICHELIN
BILSTEIN
FACOM

Newly-crowned World Champion Timo Salonen carried competition number 1 on the 1986 Monte Carlo Rally, where he finished second overall.

This was not only Kankkunen's debut win for Peugeot, but his very first victory in Europe (his first World victories had been recorded in East and West Africa respectively!). It was also the event in which Ford's RS200 finally made its bow, with ex-Peugeot driver Kalle Grundel finishing third, and setting five fastest stage times and 15 other 'podium' placings.

Then came Portugal, and that awful day when unruly spectators spilled out on to the track on an early stage, where Santos' Ford RS200 crashed on the very first stage at Sintra, killing three spectators and injuring others. Even before this, Peugeot team leader Timo Salonan's T16 E2 had been damaged when he hit the equipment of a camera team on the outside of a fast bend, and this had torn off the entire rear end of the Peugeot's bodywork.

The organisers, it seemed, had lost all control of the

Bruno Saby was never the luckiest of the Peugeot T16 works drivers, and was often overshadowed by his more illustrious team-mates. Although he set several fastest stage times on the 1986 Monte Carlo (this car), he eventually took sixth place.

Juha Kankkunen joined the Peugeot team for 1986, and almost immediately recorded his first victory – in Sweden in February.

Carefully worked over by the Todt/de Cortanze team, the E2 looked right from any angle, its aerodynamic performance being much more satisfactory than that of the original car.

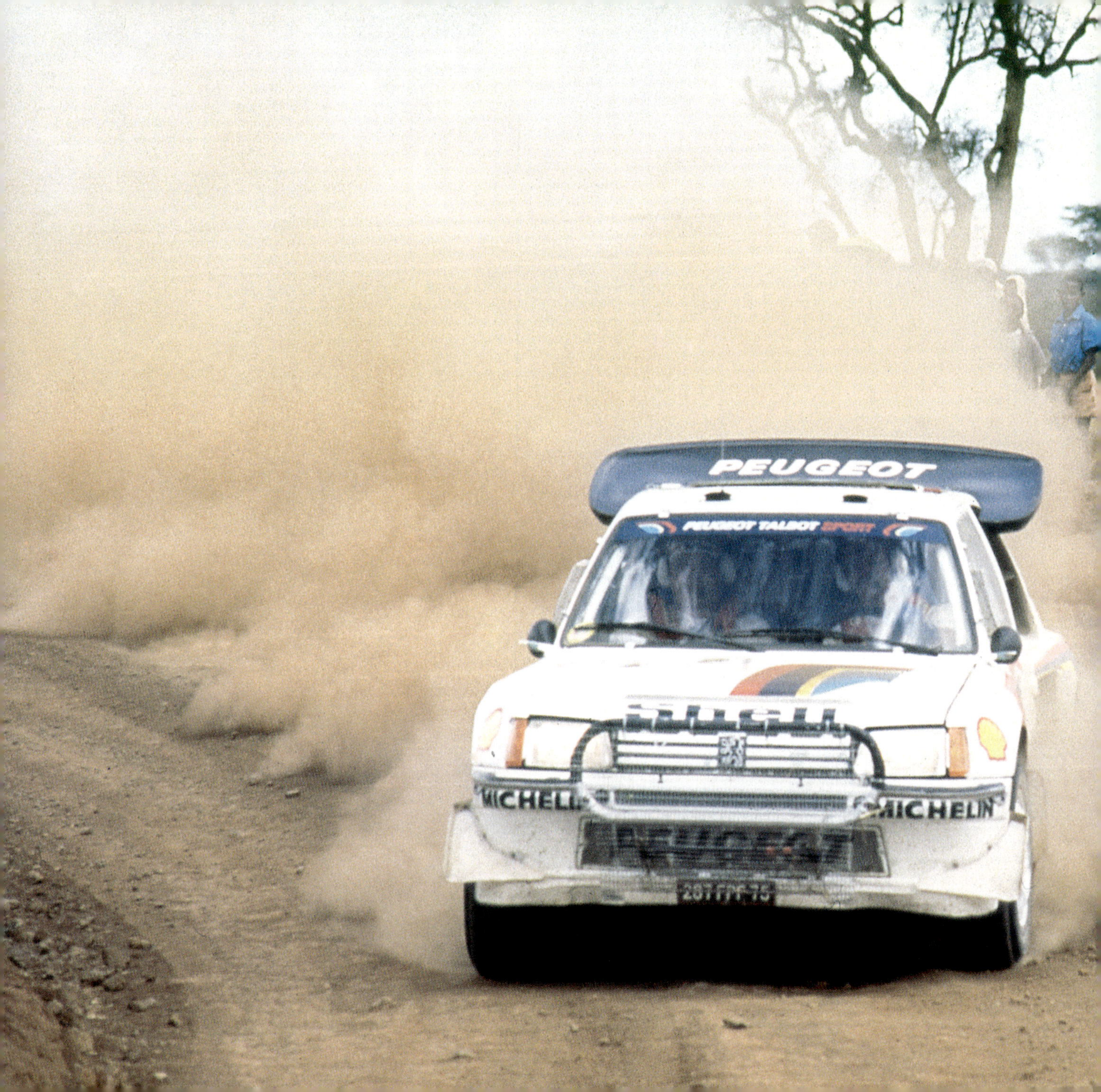
PEUGEOT
PEUGEOT TALBOT SPORT
MICHELIN
MICHELIN

Peugeot struggled to be competitive in the East African Safari in 1985 and in 1986. This was one of the 1986 E2 team cars. Juha Kankkunen took fifth place in the event.

crowds, the drivers hated the very idea of rallying through such seething masses, and as this all seemed to be too much for the works teams, they withdrew en masse. No fewer than nine A-rated drivers (including Salonen and Kankkunen) returned to Estoril, and refused to go any further. Amid all this grim drama, Peugeot's use of side skirts on the T16 E2s went almost unnoticed – but these were to be involved in yet another scandal a few months later.

Three weeks later Peugeot sent two brand-new new heavyweight T16 E2s (C212 and C214) to tackle the East African Safari (these were loaded with all the modifications that Peugeot knew they needed following the breakdowns of 1985, and the extensive testing which had been carried out early in the year in Africa), though the Lancia team, who were not yet sure of the strength of their latest four-wheel drive machine, opted to send their obsolete rear-drive Rally 037 coupés for the very last time (one cynical observer, sure that this would be a waste of time, suggested that Lancia was "getting rid of the empties ...").

Toyota, of course, sent three powerful rear-drive Celica Twin Cam Turbos – which might have looked obsolete, but as these were cars which had already won

103

Four-wheel drive

For many years, four-wheel drive cars were not eligible to enter international rallies. Even so, occasional events (such as Britain's Scottish) bent the rules to allow the Army to enter Land Rovers, but that was just for fun – not that it mattered too much, for these were slow. Up until the end of the 1970s, the only four-wheel drive private car to go on sale was the British Jensen FF, which was at once too expensive, too heavy and too precious even to be considered.

Audi then let it be known that it was considering the use of four-wheel drive for one version of a new model (which became the Coupé). The Audi team was already competing in rallies with front-wheel drive 80s, and suggested that if it was allowed to use four-wheel drive then it might get a lot more serious about motorsport.

This was only one influence, but it helped. Accordingly, the FIA authorised the use of four-wheel drive machines from 1 January 1979, and it seems that the very first 4WD cars to start an international rally were two Subarus and a Range Rover, in the East African Safari of 1980.

That, on its own, was of no significance – but the arrival of the turbocharged, four-wheel drive, Audi Quattro in 1980 most certainly was. Audi made it clear that it was going to attack the World Championships, starting in 1981, won its first event early in that year, and soon became dominant.

Once the Quattro began winning (but not, it seems, before then), several manufacturers decided that they had to follow suit. Peugeot moved faster than almost anyone else, by showing the first 205 T16 in 1983, and winning its first World rally with that car in 1984. By the mid-1980s the revolution was complete, and no two-wheel drive car has truly been competitive since then.

the Safari on two previous occasions they were seen as a real threat: Kankkunen, who had piloted the winning car in 1985, knew what he had to face. Even so, several other teams (including Peugeot's commercial partner, Citroën) did not even send cars to compete in Africa ...

Peugeot's meticulous preparations, incidentally, were well-and-truly disrupted when five-times winner Shekhar Mehta was given a car for pre-event testing, found that it burst into flames soon after his work began, after which he had to watch it completely burning out. It was easy enough for observers to be cynical, and to say that Peugeot could afford such a mishap (and, maybe they could – and, thank goodness, there had been no personal injuries), but it was an omen as to what was to follow.

And so it turned out. On an event still seen as the toughest, roughest, dustiest and most specialised of all World rally contenders, it was Bjorn Waldegård in the theoretically obsolete old-type rear-drive Toyota who led the event from start to finish, with his team-mate Lars-Erik Torph in second place throughout. Markku Alen's rear-drive Lancia took third place in the last-ever works appearance by this car (a good way, therefore, to get rid of the empties!), yet the best that a Peugeot could achieve was Juha Kankkunen's fifth place, after a late-event breakdown which could only be rectified when the Peugeot 'chase' car finally found him in the bush, miles from civilisation in Kenya. Many of Peugeot's delays were caused by the battering, the heat and the dust which uniquely afflicted cars in Kenya at Eastertime.

Worse than that was that Juha's Peugeot ended up no less than 2hr 6min off the winning pace, while Shekhar Mehta, in the other T16, took eighth place, 3hr 6min slower than the winning Toyota. Jean Todt, however, well-knew the old adage that usually no-one wins the Safari until their third attempt – and at the time vowed to make that come true in 1987. However, he would never get the chance.

The Tour de Corse, which followed in May, was a tragedy of massive scale – not only for poor Henri Toivonen and his co-driver Sergio Cresto, who were killed in a high-speed crash of colossal proportions, but for the whole of rallying, as the authorities immediately put the technically exciting

Group B category under sentence of death. Although it was announced that the cars would continue to be eligible until the end of the season, that would be the end of it all, which meant that high-tech cars like the Peugeot would be rendered obsolete.

Having tested and practised for weeks on the island, Peugeot had turned up in Corsica with three state-of-the-art T16 E2s, two of them brand new (for Salonen and Michele Mouton), along with C209 – Salonen's ex-Sweden car – for Bruno Saby, and for the first time they all had the use of specially-developed six-speed transmissions. For this all-tarmac round, the cars were hunkered down as far as possible, with side strakes under the sills, Juha Kankkunen was officially 'rested' for this event – it was known that he did not enjoy tarmac rallying, and for a time was concentrating on testing instead – but he would be back.

This high-profile event was also one which Lancia desperately wanted to win, so there were three Delta S4s entered. Run at a furious pace throughout, which meant that the tyres sometimes overheated in the sweltering Mediterranean conditions, it soon developed into a straight fight between Bruno Saby's Peugeot and Henri Toivonen's Lancia, after Timo Salonen's T16 E2 crashed on the first day after setting two fastest stage times in seven stages and Michele Mouton's car broke its transmission (which was a very rare failing for this mechanically robust Peugeot model, though this was the new six-speeder, don't forget).

After two of the three days, Toivonen was almost three minutes ahead of Saby (who loved the tight and winding tarmac roads of Corsica), and could therefore have eased off without danger of being caught. In 16 completed stages he had been fastest 12 times – it was as emphatic as that. But it was not to be. On stage 18, and to quote Martin Holmes' *World Rallying 9*: "... he flew off the road at a tightening left hand bend, the car flipped 270 degrees in the air and exploded as the bottom hit trees close to the edge of the road ... The following competitors were sent directly to Calvi and no attempt was made to run the remaining stages that day.

"The rest of the event became a procession and Bruno Saby did not feel he could properly celebrate his first World Championship victory ..."

Neither could Peugeot. On the third and final day, Saby's car was the only truly competitive works car still in the event, and at the finish his winning margin had risen to a massive 14 minutes, which could never reflect the competition of the first two legs, or, of course, of the tragic consequences of Toivonen's crash. The fact that this hollow victory in Corsica gave the Peugeot team a lead in the World Championship which they were never to lose (and that, in fact, it spurred them on to take four further victories in the rest of the season) was quite lost in the sombre mood which prevailed in rallying in the summer months.

The FIA immediately announced a ban on Group B from the end of the year, and, in the same announcement, banned the use of under-body skirts. Audi immediately withdrew from rallying, Ford immediately ran down their development efforts in Group B, Austin-Rover and Citroën both faded from the competitive scene, and before long the balance of the 1986 season became a straight fight between Peugeot and Lancia. It was predictable that Lancia's morale suffered badly after the horrors of Corsica, such that they only won one more event in 1986 – Argentina – for their politically dubious efforts to win at home, in San Remo, were eventually foiled by officialdom.

In an extraordinary press conference held after the end of the Tour de Corse, Peugeot's Chairman, Jean Boillot, vowed to keep his team in motorsport, commenting that: "I believe that all motorsports are dangerous, but we must eliminate as much of the danger as we can. You can never achieve complete safety, however ...

"Rally sport improves the image which brings results and new customers..."

For Peugeot, the battle in the next round, the Acropolis in Greece was not as much against Lancia as in raising its spirits (and, by inference) that of rallying once again. It was also against physical damage to tyres, cars, undersides and transmissions, and the amazing fact is that two of the three works T16 E2 cars (all being 'previously used' – two of them having started, and briefly competed, in Portugal) made it to

Bruno Saby took a fine third place in the 1986 Acropolis Rally, that event being won by Juha Kankkunen in a sister car.

the finish. This time it was the Ford RS200s which matched the Peugeots until a series of mechanical misfortunes overtook the British cars, for the only Lancia to stay on terms was that of Miki Biasion: his team-mate, Markku Alen, was fast, but had to over-stress his Lancia's transmission, then its engine, to take fastest times, so it rewarded him by blowing up within three stages of the finish.

For Peugeot, it was the two loose-surface specialists, Juha Kankkunen and Timo Salonen, who swapped a series of fastest and 'podium' fast times, until Salonen hit one very hard part of Greece so severely that the entire chassis of his T16 E2 was badly bent, and he eventually had to retire – it is interesting to look down the list of Peugeot's cars and to see that that particular chassis number was not used again!

That was the bad news – the good news being that Kankkunen eventually won the event (from Biasion's Lancia) by just 97 seconds, while the modest Saby kept going well, never quite as rapidly (he didn't set a single fastest stage time), but equally as consistently, and finally took third place.

The World Championship then took a short break before Peugeot and Lancia (but no other serious works

The Coventry connection

Although Peugeot now claims that the engineering of the 205 T16 was almost entirely an in-house project, based on Peugeot factories in France, some of the practical, side-of-the-road, advice initially came from its Talbot Sunbeam-Lotus works team in Coventry, England.

Way back in the 1950s, 1960s and 1970s, the Rootes Group built up a mountain of rallying expertise, and success, with Sunbeams (and, in the London-Sydney Marathon, with the Hillman Hunter). Rootes then became Chrysler, Chrysler sold out to Peugeot in 1978, and in 1979 Peugeot revived the once-famous 'Talbot' brand for its cars.

Des O'Dell, who was managing the company's motorsport efforts in Coventry, and was needing a rally winner, set out to do it on the 'wing-and-a-prayer' basis: "If I was to beat the Escorts," he once told me, "I needed to build a better Escort, so that is what I did …"

Starting on the basis of the Chrysler (later 'Talbot') Sunbeam hatchback, he built a prototype with a Lotus 16-valve engine, and a ZF five-speed gearbox, and somehow persuaded top management to see it put into production. Thus, the Chrysler (later 'Talbot') Sunbeam-Lotus was born, and became the company's front-line rally car in 1980.

Jean Todt became works driver Guy Frequelin's co-driver in those years, the two notching up a third and a fourth place, while Henri Toivonen won the British RAC Rally. In 1981, not only did Frequelin/Todt finish second in the Drivers' Championship (with one victory and three second places), but the team also won the Makes Championship outright.

As this was achieved on what passed for a shoestring budget in those days, Peugeot was duly impressed, and when Jean Todt was appointed as motorsport director, and tasked with building a new Group B car, he spent much time consulting the Coventry operation on all practical matters.

Juha Kankkunen in his works 205 T16 E2, on his way to winning the 1986 Rally of New Zealand. Kankkunen would become World Champion in that season.

Timo Salonen's T16 E2 jumps straight and true on the 1000 Lakes in 1986 – which was his second 1000 Lakes success, and the third Finnish victory for the T16.

One of the visual features of the T16 E2 was its extra aerodynamic fittings – especially the front trim tabs, and the vast rear spoiler. These helped to ensure that it would fly straight and level over high-speed jumps.

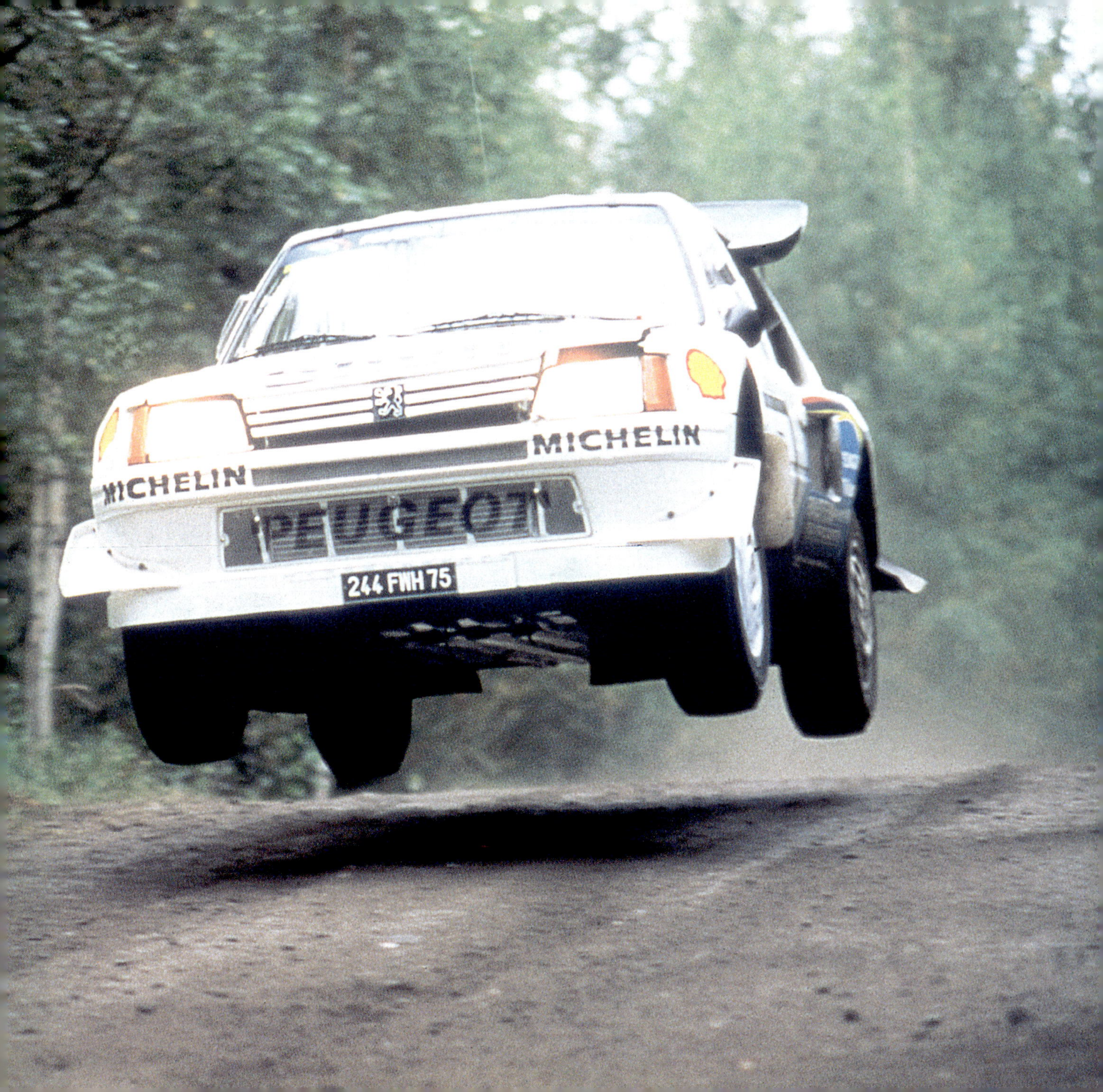
MICHELIN
MICHELIN
PEUGEOT
244 FWH 75

Timo Salonen, sideways on the way into a tight corner in Finland in 1986, when he won the 1000 Lakes Rally.

T16 hit a Japanese private owner on a liaison section.

As for Juha and Markku, both were quick and both were decisive, though Juha did not really begin to pull away until the last day, when he finally stretched his lead to 100 seconds. For every other team, it was ominous that none of these highly-tuned works cars retired, or broke anything significant: perhaps it was well that their proposed developments for 1987 could never now been seen, for both teams would surely have had 500+bhp monsters which would have made all previous rally cars look positively slow.

In Argentina, as in New Zealand, the big battle was between three Peugeots and three Lancias – though this time it was Lancia's turn to take a victory – only its second (the first had been in Monte Carlo), and as it happened, its last of the 1986 season. With Timo Salonen not willing to go to Argentina (somehow or other he convinced Jean Todt that he needed a holiday, and was granted it), Peugeot 'borrowed' an out-of-work Stig Blomqvist from Ford, and re-fettled three already-used cars – two from New Zealand, and one for Bruno Saby which was the same chassis he had used in the Acropolis.

Strangely, Lancia seemed to be in total control throughout the event – predictably, perhaps, it had taken them so long to bounce back from the traumas of Corsica – for Miki Biaison led the event almost from flag drop to finish. Even so, the list of stage times show that it was Markku Alen's Lancia which set more fastest times, and the best of

teams – they had been terminally disheartened by the events of Corsica) arrived in Auckland in July, for the Rally of New Zealand. It was a time in which Peugeot once again made its displeasure with the authorities very clear indeed (there was no love lost between Peugeot's Jean Todt and FISA's fiery president, Jean-Marie Balestre), for by this time the company had worked out the financial penalties it was going to have to face because of the cancellation of Group B – and it wanted recompense. Not that it got any, not even in the French courts, but its relations with FISA were soured for years as a consequence.

In New Zealand, two brand new T16 E2s (chassis nos 217 and 218) faced up to three Lancia Delta S4s, and it was a measure of their pace that no other car ever looked like breaking in among their ranks. All five of those cars started and all finished in top five positions. However, although Peugeot fielded both Kankkunen and Timo Salonen, it was always Kankkunen who fought it out for the lead with Markku Alen, though Timo Salonen could hardly be blamed for a delay caused by repairing collision damage after his the Peugeots (Kankkunen and Blomqvist) could record only two fastest times each. Amazingly (for the T16 E2 was now usually considered to be a very reliable machine), two of the Peugeots retired – Kankkunen's with a collapsed rear suspension strut, which immobilised him, and Saby's car with a broken engine. Blomqvist, who might have been an ex-World Champion, but on this occasion was no more than a 'substitute', finished third, and helped keep Peugeot ahead in the race for Makes Championship points.

With the World Championship now no more than a two-make race (Austin-Rover was still involved, but the ugly Metro 6R4s were being outpaced by Peugeot and Lancia), in Finland the event became a high-speed gravel road-race between three Peugeots (just one of them, for Salonen, being brand-new) and the usual three Lancias. For Peugeot, Timo Salonen, Juha Kankkunen and Stig Blomqvist faced up to Lancia's Markku Alen, Michael Ericsson and Kalle Grundel, and no excuses were being made by either side.

Although Markku Alen, on home ground, threw down the gauntlet to all his rivals, and led the event until the last morning, both teams had produced ultra-fast, ultra-reliable cars for this very high-speed event. Off-road incidents, accidents and other dramas were all otherwise overcome, and it wasn't until Alen's Lancia went off the road for a short time that Timo Salonen took the lead – looking for his first outright victory of the season. Even so, it was all very close, right to the end: Salonen's 14 fastest stage times were outpaced by Alen's 27 fastest times, but by sheer consistency alone Timo won by just 24 seconds from Juha Kankkunen in the second of the Peugeots, with Alen's Lancia third and the ever reliable Blomqvist fourth in the third Peugeot.

Then came San Remo – home conditions for Lancia, where naturally it was expected to start as favourite – and what followed was a real scandal. Even before the event started, a miasma of distrust was apparent in Italy, where the Press, ever loyal to its own, had cast Peugeot as cheating villains. The fact that the French cars turned up with super-powerful engines, and immediately began to humiliate Lancia's efforts on its home ground, did not help.

This is what rallying's doyen Martin Homes, had to say in his *World Rallying 9*, which appeared at the end of the season: "For reasons never admitted or explained, Italian scrutineers claimed the works Peugeot cars were fitted with illegal under-car pieces and the Sporting Stewards were persuaded these pieces had been fitted fraudulently, which meant that the cars had to be banned immediately from continuing in the event.

"It was a drastic act of vendetta against the French cars, whose only fault in Italian eyes had been to be faster than the Italian cars on the early asphalt sections ..."

In fact, the T16 E2s were running in a similar specification to that seen in recent appearances on the World Championship scene, where there had been no problems, and no complaints from other teams, or from the scrutineers on these events. The only difference on this occasion was that they were now running on Italian soil – captive, as it were – where an Italian rival stood to gain from a disqualification, and where summary justice could be handed out.

To most neutral (in other words, non-Italian) observers, the disqualification of the Peugeots was totally wrong. As *Autosport's* Peter Foubister wrote: "To most, it was an outrageous move with no real credibility ..."

Before scandal hit the headlines, Peugeot's four works cars (this time including a car for Andrea Zanussi) had begun by humiliating the Lancias, and, naturally, the MG Metro 6R4s, and it was only when the event moved on to gravel stages that the Lancias could fight back. Even so, by the time the field reached the night halt at Pisa, Juha Kankkunen's 205 T16 E2 was well and truly in the lead. In the meantime, the organisers had seen the timing of one special stage descend into chaos – and it just so happened that the contender to suffer most from errors was Zanussi driving a Peugeot, which might have been a coincidence but ...

Eventually, and without making any allowances for appeal, at the end of the third of four legs (with just seven stages to go, and where the Lancias could not possibly have closed the gaps) the 205s were summarily ejected.

"The elimination of the Peugeots happened like clockwork, in best Italian style," wrote Martin Holmes.

Anyone who doubted the use of four-wheel drive should study the grip being developed by every wheel on this works E2 on a gravel surface.

"Nobody knew who gave the orders, and when it was all over the times on stage 22 were cancelled without demur ..."

For the time being, it seemed, Peugeot was in disgrace, but within weeks the situation had been reversed, leaving the San Remo Rally's reputation in tatters instead, and Lancia without anything to celebrate. Protest at the highest level led to FISA completely annulling the results of the event in December 1986, so Peugeot got its 'phantom' victory after all, though it was never to count for World Championship points. And were the organisers ashamed of themselves, or penalised in future? It seems not, for San Remo was back in the World series in the following year. It was almost as if such scandal, and such sleaze, had never occurred.

For Jean Todt and Peugeot, there were just two events remaining where they could give Lancia another thrashing – the first of these being the long (45 special stages) four-day RAC Rally of Great Britain. After San Remo it was no more than poetic justice that the Peugeots won the event (Timo Salonen was the driver), also taking third and fourth placings, while Markku Alen's Lancia was second.

Because Group B was imminently approaching closure, for the French it was really a case of 'using up old stock', so all three cars in the event had previous history: Salonen's car, for instance, had already taken third in Argentina and fifth in New Zealand. Although the battle with Lancias was as intense as expected – at the end of the event, the winning margin was only 82 seconds – both Kankkunen and Salonen took turns to lead, between them sharing no fewer than 20 fastest stage times.

Now for the final shoot out, early in December in

PEUGEOT
PEUGEOT TALBOT
Shell
MICHELIN
aerospatiale
MICHELIN
709 EXC 75

Maybe we can't always trust registration numbers, but 319FPF75 adorned the cars which won the 1986 Acropolis, Rally of New Zealand and Lombard-RAC rallies, as driven by Juha Kankkunen and Timo Salonen.

the Olympus Rally of the USA, which was an event which flared only briefly on the World scene. At the time of this rally the fraudulent results of the San Remo event still stood, so Peugeot needed to go to the USA for Juha Kankkunen and the 205 T16 to get all the points they could. It was not until ten days later – after the Olympus – that the authorities abruptly annulled San Remo, making everyone's trip an expensive waste of time.

Expensive, for sure – the event was held in Washington state, on the far west coast of the USA – so Peugeot sent just one 205 T16 for Kankkunen, while Lancia sent a single Delta for Markku Alen. The only other credible competition came from Toyota, which sent a full team of three two-wheel drive Celica TCTs, though the Japanese can surely not have hoped for better than minor placings.

By Group B rallying standards, this particular Peugeot was quite an old hack (though meticulously prepared). Carrying chassis number C218, it had first appeared in New Zealand (Kankkunen, won the event), then in Argentina (Kankkunen, broken suspension), and in San Remo (Kankkunen, disqualified while leading).

This time round, victory went to the Lancia team without controversy, for although the Peugeot led at first, Alen's car took over on stage 7, and gradually pulled away. Even so, Kankkunen set 20 fastest stage times to the Lancia's 23 fastest times, and no other driver even got a look in. After three days, the winning margin was a sturdy 3min 26sec and honour – if such a word still applied to World rallying at the time – seemed to be satisfied,

At which point the curtain came down, firmly and irrevocably, on Peugeot's Group B rally programme. Ten days later FISA formally annulled the San Remo, the revised points tables showed that Peugeot had once again won the Manufacturers' Championship, and that Juha Kankkunen had become World Driver's Champion. In the meantime, Peugeot sued the authorities for a minimum of £3 million over losses incurred by the cancellation of Group B – though after the usually lengthy legal delays the action failed.

Although Peugeot-Talbot Sport remained in being, and would continue as a major power in rallying, sportscar racing and, eventually, in the field of F1 engine supply, Jean Todt's ultra-successful Group B Operation was no more. After just one year with the team, his newly-crowned World Champion, Juha Kankkunen, went off to drive for Lancia in 1987 (where he would once again become World Champion), while Timo Salonen moved to the Mazda team for 1987, where he won one event (Sweden), but otherwise had an unsuccessful year. Bruno Saby drove three times for Lancia, but did not shine again.

With no useful afterlife ahead of them, the existing works

This symbolic picture shows a 205 T16 E2, out on its own – which was the situation Peugeot created for itself in many events in 1984, 1985 and 1986. The car's career was only cut off by an abrupt change of rules which came at the end of 1986.

fleet of 205 T16 E2s were gradually sold off, turned into rally cross cars, loaned out to museums and collections, or just stored. Because Group B had been killed off, there was really no alternative use for such specialised machinery.

Unless, that is, your name was Jean Todt, and you saw an opportunity of winning yet more honours – in the desert ...

Well before the end of the year, Peugeot made it clear that attentions would be turn to major 'Raid' rallies in the desert, especially to the prestigious Paris-Dakar event which would end on the Atlantic coast in January. The car chosen (which has already been described in the 'Car and the team' section, was the 205 T16 Grand Raid model – longer, heavier, even more robust, and with a colossal fuel tank – which would become quite dominant in this type of event in the next few years.

The 205 T16's successor

Because the FIA had cancelled the Group B category so abruptly – the announcement came in May, which gave companies like Peugeot only seven more months in which to capitalise on their technical and financial investment – and because the 205 T16 was still not at the height of its powers, by the end of 1986 Peugeot had not so far troubled to start the development of a new model to replace the T16. In any case, Peugeot and team boss Jean Todt were so incensed by the FIA's dictatorial move (because it had been taken under their noses, in Paris, and without any consultation, by an organisation whose President was French, they felt doubly hurt) that they elected to have nothing more to do with World-level rallying for the foreseeable future.

Apart from this being a knee-jerk reaction, with an element of pique built in to the withdrawal, there was also much Gallic logic involved as well. Because rallying in the late 1980s was going to be for very powerful Group A cars, with four-wheel drive transmission (rear-wheel drive cars had, at the most, two years before they were rendered obsolete), this meant that a competitive rally team already had to have access to such a production machine, which needed to be on sale, and of which more than 5000 had already been produced.

Lancia (with its Delta HF 4WD) was obviously sitting pretty, Ford's Sierra XR4x4 looked promising (it took time for Ford to realise what an awful engine that car was actually lumbered with), while Audi's normally aspirated Coupé Quattro and Mazda's 323 4WD were also handily placed. Peugeot, on the other hand, had nothing to offer and nothing in prospect. Not a single model in its 1987 product range had four-wheel drive (and no such installation, it seems, was even planned), its front-drive 205s were all under-powered, and its larger 505s were too heavy. Even if Todt had persuaded the company to carry on, it would have taken at least three years for a new derivative of any existing Peugeot to be developed, and such a delay was unthinkable.

Accordingly, the 205 T16 did not have a direct rallying successor, though the 205 T16 'Grand Raid', and the 405 T16 which followed it, became supreme in long-distance events in Africa, and used much of the engineering of the earlier model.

In the meantime, Jean Todt's Peugeot-Talbot Sport operation turned its attention to long-distance sportscar racing where Porsche and Jaguar were currently dominant. Predictably, it eventually enjoyed great success with the 905 two-seater, and then went on to develop 3.5-litre V10 Formula 1 engines for supply to companies like McLaren (which was by no means as competitive). After Todt left the company (he became Ferrari's much-acclaimed F1 team boss, and built up a revitalised team around Michael Schumacher), rallying, as a sport at Peugeot, was almost completely ignored for the rest of the 1990s.

Accordingly, it was well over a decade before Peugeot once again turned its attention to rallying, and to the design of a competitive World Rally Car. This, the 206WRC, started winning in 2000, and became just as successful as the 205 T16 had ever been.

Visit Veloce on the web – www.veloce.co.uk
Details of all books in print • Special offers • New book news • Gift vouchers

World Rally success

Event	Position	Car	Drivers
1984			
1000 Lakes	1st	704EXC75	A Vatanen/T Harryman
San Remo	1st	128FBL75	A Vatanen/T Harryman
RAC	1st	128FBL75	A Vatanen/T Harryman
1985			
Monte Carlo	1st	716EXC75	A Vatanen/T Harryman
Monte Carlo	3rd	323EXA75	T Salonen/S Harjanne
Sweden	1st	716EXC75	A Vatanan/T Harryman
Sweden	3rd	323EXA75	T Salonen/S Harjanne
Portugal	1st	323EXA75	T Salonen/S Harjanne
Tour de Corse	2nd	24FGV75	B Saby/J-F Fauchille
Acropolis	1st	25FGV75	T Salonen/S Harjanne
New Zealand	1st	704EXC75	T Salonen/S Harjanne
New Zealand	2nd	123FBL75	A Vatanen/T Harryman
Argentina	1st	704EXC75	T Salonen/S Harjanne
Argentina	3rd	709EXC75	C Reutemann/J-F Fauchille
1000 Lakes	1st	704EXC 75	T Salonen/S Harjanne
San Remo	2nd	704EXC75	T Salonen/S Harjanne
1986			
Monte Carlo	2nd	24FGV75	T Salonen/S Harjanne
Sweden	1st	26FGV75	J Kankkunen/J Piironen
Tour de Corse	1st	239FWH75	B Saby/J-F Fauchille
Acropolis	1st	319FPF75	J Kankkunen/J Piironen
Acropolis	3rd	290FPF75	B Saby/J-F Fauchille
New Zealand	1st	319FPF75	J Kankkunen/J Piironen
Argentina	3rd	311FPF75	S Blomqvist/B Berglund
1000 Lakes	1st	237FWH75	T Salonen/S Harjanne
1000 Lakes	2nd	239FWH75	J Kankkunen/J Piironen

Event	Position	Car	Drivers
1986 continued			
San Remo	Fraudulently disqualified when leading the event before the final day's stages.	319FPF75	J Kankkunen/J Piironen
RAC	1st	319FPF75	T Salonen/S Harjanne
RAC	3rd	237FWH75	J Kankkunen/J Piironen
Olympus (USA)	2nd	294FPF75	J Kankkunen/J Piironen

Works rally cars (and when first used)

These are the identities (by registration number, all of them originating in Paris) of the factory-prepared Peugeot 205 T16 rally cars built and registered by Peugeot in France between 1984 and 1986, for use in major World events. As bodyshells wore out, or after a serious crash, some of these identities may have been 'cloned' on to newly-built cars. Where applicable, I have added important successes. Note: Peugeot, like other manufacturers of this period, swapped registration plates from car to car, sometimes more than once, so it may not be safe to assume that a particular identity was always the same car !

1984
323EXA75 (3rd, 1985 Monte Carlo)
697EXC75
704EXC75 (1st, 1984 1000 Lakes; 1st, 1985 New Zealand; 1st, 1985 Argentina; 1st, 1985, 1000 Lakes; 2nd, 1985 San Remo)
709EXC75 (3rd, 1985 Argentina)
716EXC75 (1st, 1985 Monte Carlo)
123FBL75 (2nd, 1985 New Zealand)
128FBL75 (1st, 1984 San Remo; 1st, 1984 RAC)

1985
24FGV75 (2nd, 1985 Tour de Corse; 2nd, 1986 Monte Carlo)
25FGV75 (1st, 1985 Acropolis)
26FGV75 (1st, 1986 Sweden)

1986
287FPF75
290FPF75 (3rd, 1986 Acropolis)
294FPF75 (2nd, 1986 Olympus)
311FPF75 (3rd, 1986 Argentina)
319FPF75 (1st, 1986 Acropolis; 1st, 1986 New Zealand; 1st, 1986 RAC)
237FWH75 (1st, 1986 1000 Lakes; 3rd, 1986 RAC)
239FWH75 (1st, 1986 Tour de Corse; 2nd, 1986 1000 Lakes)
244FWH75

Note: Like other works teams of the period, Peugeot was quite ready to swap registration numbers from one chassis to another – and sometimes did so.
According to a list provided to rally historian Martin Holmes in 1986, the works team identified their chassis by C-numbers, and unveiled them as follows:

1983:   P1

1984:   C1, C2, C3, C4, C5, C6 and C7

1985:   C8, C9, C10, C11, C12, C15, C16, C17, C18, C19 and C20
(Second evolution cars) C201, C202, C203, C204

1986:   C13
(Second evolution cars) C206, C207, C208, C209, C210, C211, C212, C214, C215, C216, C217, C218, C219
In addition, chassis numbered M1 and P4 were used for test/training in 1984, as was P200 in 1985, and C213 in 1986. All in all, that makes a total of 41 cars (of which, 19 were second evolution machines) – which is a lot more than the 18 registration numbers I have identified. Pity the poor historian!

All 200 road cars were completed in this sombre, but very purposeful colour scheme.

£24.99* • ISBN 978-1-845841-15-7

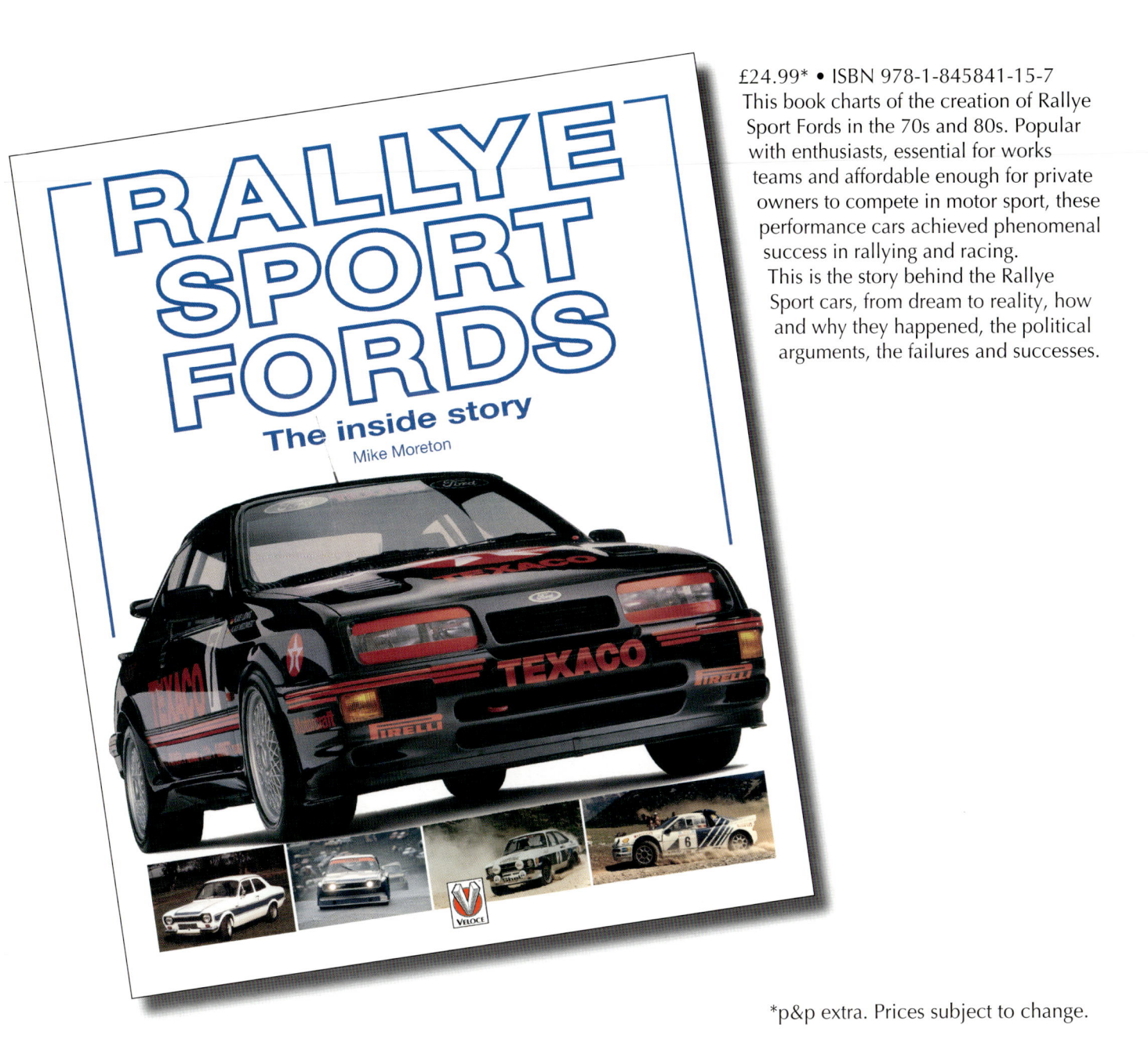

This book charts of the creation of Rallye Sport Fords in the 70s and 80s. Popular with enthusiasts, essential for works teams and affordable enough for private owners to compete in motor sport, these performance cars achieved phenomenal success in rallying and racing.

This is the story behind the Rallye Sport cars, from dream to reality, how and why they happened, the political arguments, the failures and successes.

*p&p extra. Prices subject to change.

£14.99* • ISBN 978-1-845840-40-2
This book describes the birth, development, and rallying career of the original Ford Escort, one of Europe's landmark rally cars, in the early 1970s, providing a compact and authoritative history of where, how and why it became so important to the sport.

£14.99* • ISBN 978-1-845841-28-7
This book describes the birth, development, and rallying career of the Austin Healey, listing each and every success and notable car, tracing exactly how the machinery developed, and improved, from one season to the next.
It provides a compact and authoritative history of where, how and why it became so important to the sport.

*p&p extra. Prices subject to change.

Index

Note : There are so many mentions of the 205 T16 (also coded M24-Rally) and its evolution, the T16 Grand Raid, on individual pages, that it is impractical to Index them.

A
Alen, Markku 74, 81, 98, 104, 106, 110-112, 114
Alpine-Renault (and models) 26, 57
Aston Martin (and models) 57
Audi (and models) 7, 9, 14-16, 27, 29, 35, 37, 64, 72, 74-77, 79, 81, 84, 92, 96-98, 104, 105, 116
Austin-Rover (and models) 17, 35, 42, 97, 105, 111
Autosport 79, 111

B
Balestre, Jean-Marie 110
Bettega, Attilio 71
Biasion, Miki 106, 110
Blomqvist, Stig 72, 74, 84, 92, 96, 110
BMW (and models) 33
Boillot, Jean 15, 105

C
Chambers, Marcus 57
Chrysler (UK and Europe, and models) 13-15, 18, 22, 107
Citroën (and models) 8, 16, 27, 28, 30, 32, 35, 64, 72, 104, 105
Clark, Roger 9
Cortanze, Andre de 37, 38, 41, 43, 79, 92, 101
Cosworth 17, 27, 57
Coventry-Climax 33
Cresto, Sergio 104

D
Datsun (and models) 60
DeLorean (and models) 26
Dixon, Freddie 33

E
Ericsson, Michael 111

F
Ferguson, Harry 33
Ferrari (and models) 8, 9, 55
FF Developments (FFD, and Harry Ferguson Research) 32, 33
FIA (and FISA) 10, 22, 35, 62, 104, 105, 110, 112, 115, 116
Fiat (and models) 9, 10, 60
Ford (and models) 9, 13, 15, 17, 27, 32, 33, 35, 42, 54, 57, 61, 64, 71, 74, 79, 97, 98, 100, 105, 110, 116
Foubister, Peter 79, 111

G
Gallagher, Fred 97
General Motors 35
Ghia 17

H
Hillman (and models) 15, 57
Holmes, Martin 72, 105, 111

J
Jaguar (and models) 116
Jensen (and models) 33, 104
Jones, Mick 79

L
Lancia (and models) 9, 15, 17, 35, 37, 40, 42, 45, 61, 71, 74-77, 81, 96-98, 103-106, 110-112, 114-116
Land Rover 104
Lotus (and models) 14, 15, 32

123

M
Mazda (and models) 61, 115, 116
McLaren 116
MG (and models) 17, 32, 37, 97, 98, 111
Michelin (test track at Clermont Ferrand) 46
Mikkola, Hannu 9, 84
Mitsubishi (and models) 57
Moncet, Jean-Louis 30
Motor Shows :
   Geneva 26

N
Nissan (and models) 35, 60, 61, 75, 81, 85
Nowicki, Nick 9

O
O'Dell, Des 12, 13, 15, 21, 23, 24, 26, 29, 30, 36-38, 42, 45, 53, 55, 57, 107
Opel (and models) 57, 69

P
Perron, Bernard 24, 28, 42
Peugeot 205, The Story of a Challenge 30
Peugeot factories (and workshops):
   Boulogne (Paris) 42, 62
   Coventry (ex-Chrysler-UK) 107
   Garenne-Colombes 24, 42, 62
   Mortefontaine proving grounds 18, 62
   Poissy 22, 64
   Sochaux 10, 62
   Tremery 32
Peugeot models :
   104 27, 28, 40
   204 40
   205 (also coded M24) 24, 25, 27, 29, 40, 116
   206 World Rally Car 11, 64
   304 40
   305 27
   404 9, 10, 67
   405 T16 Grand Raid 8, 39, 41, 55, 116
   504 (and V6-engined models) 10, 11, 57, 59, 67
   505 116
   604 26
   905 8, 55
Peugeot (& Peugeot Talbot) race, rally & co-drivers:
   Andersson, Ove 67, 84
   Blomqvist, Stig 110, 111
   Consten, Bernard 11
   Dacremont, Christine 11
   Fauchille, Jean-Francois 43
   Frequelin, Guy 12, 13, 107
   Grundel, Kalle 45, 96, 97, 100, 111
   Harjanne, Seppo 43, 60
   Harryman, Terry 20, 43, 57, 71, 76, 78, 80, 83, 91, 94
   Jabouille, Jean-Pierre 46
   Lampinen, Simo 54, 67
   Kankkunen, Juha 7, 8, 48, 61, 97, 98, 101, 103-107, 110-112, 114, 115
   Makinen, Timo 54
   Mehta, Shekhar 104
   Mikkola, Hannu 11, 54, 61, 67
   Mouton, Michele 46, 93, 105
   Nicolas, Jean-Pierre 7, 21, 43, 57, 59, 62, 64, 67, 69, 71, 72, 74, 77, 78, 80, 82
   Piironen, Juha 97
   Reutemann, Carlos 94, 96
   Saby, Bruno 43, 82, 83, 85, 92, 93, 97, 101, 105, 106, 110, 111, 115
   Salonen, Timo 7, 8, 43, 59, 60, 81, 83-85, 88, 92-94, 96-98, 100, 103, 105, 106, 108, 110, 112, 114, 115
   Shankland, Bert 10
   Sundstrom, Michael 45, 97
   Toivonen, Henri 12, 17
   Vatanen, Ari 7-9, 20, 36, 39, 46, 57, 61, 62, 69, 71, 72, 74-84, 87, 90, 91, 92, 94, 96, 97
   White, Paul 12
   Zanussi, Andrea 111
Pininfarina 33
Porsche (and models) 17, 35, 59, 116

R

Races (and hillclimbs):
   Le Mans 8, 55
   Pike's Peak 8, 39, 55, 57
Ragnotti, Jean 92
Rallies:
   Acropolis 48, 57, 72, 74, 92, 93, 105, 106, 110, 114
   Argentina 36, 57, 61, 82, 94, 96, 97, 110, 112
   Bandama (Ivory Coast) 10, 59, 61, 98
   Canada 60
   London-Sydney Marathon 15, 107
   Mille Pistes 21, 62
   Monte Carlo 9, 18, 46, 57, 59, 62, 80, 82, 83, 91, 92, 97, 98, 100, 101, 110
   Morocco 11, 59
   New Zealand 61, 92, 94, 106, 107, 110, 112, 114
   Olympus (USA) 112, 114
   Paris-Dakar 8, 17, 38, 40, 55, 57, 94, 116
   Portugal 46, 84, 85, 88, 100, 105
   RAC of Great Britain 12, 51, 77, 78, 80, 97, 98, 107, 112, 114
   Safari 9, 10, 41, 46, 59, 61, 67, 74, 84, 85, 88, 90, 98, 103, 104
   San Remo 40, 46, 76-78, 97, 111, 112, 114, 115
   Scottish 104
   Sweden 84, 87, 98, 101, 115
   1000 Lakes 46, 57, 60, 74-76, 92, 96, 97, 108, 109, 111
   Tour de Corse (Corsica) 17, 18, 22, 38, 40, 46, 57, 62, 68, 69, 71, 74, 92, 93, 104-106
   Trophee Francois Piot (Sarlat) Rally 62
   UDT World Cup 11
Range Rover 104
Renault (and models) 26, 54, 57, 59, 92
Ricardo 33
Rohrl, Walter 81, 84, 97
Rolt, Major Tony 33
Rootes Group 14, 57, 107

S

Sainz, Carlos 61
Santos, Joachim 100
Schumacher, Michael 8, 55, 116
Simca 14, 22
Subaru (and models) 57, 61, 104
Sunbeam (and models) 57

T

Talbot (and models) 9, 12-15, 27, 29, 42, 55, 57, 107
Todt, Jean 7, 11-15, 17, 18, 22, 23, 27, 28, 30, 40, 42, 43, 45, 53-55, 57, 59, 61, 62, 64, 66, 69, 71, 72, 74, 75, 77, 79-81, 85, 87, 92, 97, 101, 107, 110, 112, 115, 116
Toivonen, Henri 81, 98, 104, 105, 107
Torph, Lars-Erik 104
Toyota (and models) 42, 61, 75, 85, 96, 97, 103, 104, 114

V

Vaucard, Jean-Claude 28
VW (and models) 16

W

Waldegård, Bjorn 104
World Drivers' Championship 8, 40, 57, 60, 61, 107, 115
World Makes' Championship 8, 13, 15, 40, 55, 57, 62, 82, 97, 105, 107, 111, 112, 115
World Rallying 72, 105, 111

Z

Zakspeed 27

£14.99* • ISBN 978-1-84584-041-9
This book describes the birth, development, and rallying career of the Lancia Stratos, Europe's very first purpose-built rally car, in the mid/late 1970s, providing a compact and authoritative history of where, when and how it became so important to the sport.

RALLY GIANTS

Lancia
Stratos

Graham Robson

RALLY GIANTS

Subaru
Impreza

Graham Robson

£14.99* • ISBN 978-1-84584-042-6
This book describes the birth, development, and rallying car of the turbocharged, four-wheel-drive Subaru Impreza in the 1990s and early 2000s. It provides a compact and authoritative history of where, how and why it became so important to the sport.

*p&p extra. Prices subject to change.

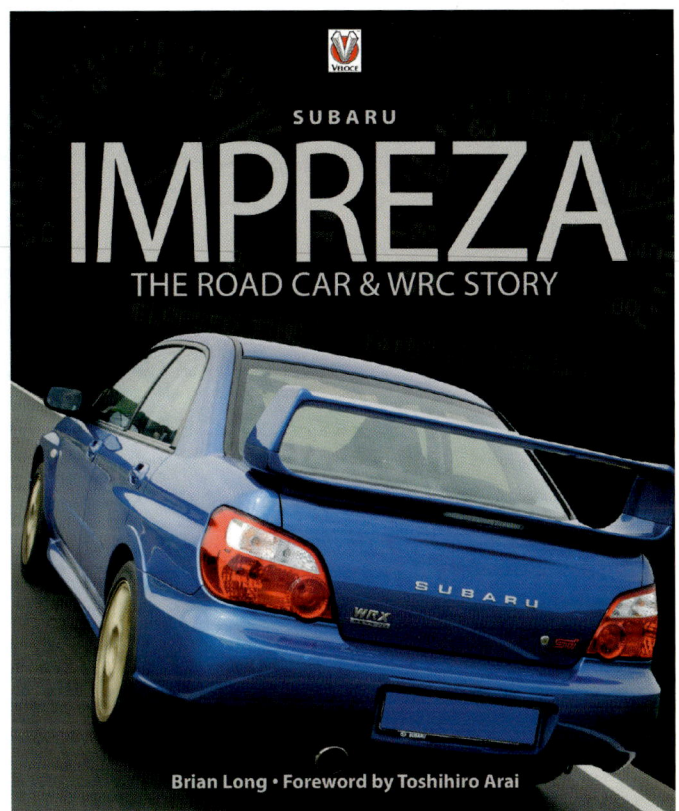

SUBARU IMPREZA
THE ROAD CAR & WRC STORY
Brian Long • Foreword by Toshihiro Arai

£29.99* hardback • ISBN 978-1-84584-028-0
£19.99* paperback • ISBN 978-1-84584-033-4

Perceived as a replacement for the long running Leone, the Impreza quickly gained a good reputation through Subaru's successful WRC programme. This book covers the full story of the Impreza, from concept through to the current production car, looking at the rally machines along the way, and illustrated throughout with contemporary material.

£29.99* hardback • ISBN 978-1-84584-055-6
£19.99* paperback • ISBN 978-1-84584-063-1

The Lancer name conjures up many images. For some, it evokes the first generation cars which fought with the best on the Safari Rally and came out the victors. Others will remember the second generation models, and who could not be aware of the Evolution (Evo) series, launched in 1992? The Lancer Evolution is not only one of the greatest rally cars of all time, it is also a desirable high-performance road car, too. Written in Japan with the full cooperation of Mitsubishi, this is the definitive story of all the world's Lancers, whether they carried Mitsubishi, Dodge, Colt, Plymouth, Valiant, Eagle, Proton or Hyundai badges.

MITSUBISHI LANCER EVO
THE ROAD CAR & WRC STORY
Brian Long • Foreword by Shinichi Kurihara

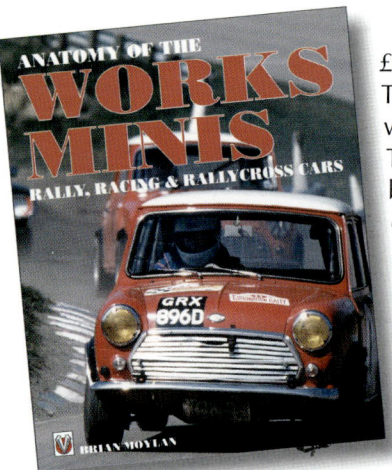

£14.99* • ISBN 978-1-903706-03-9

The inside story of how the giant-killing Minis of rallying, rallycross and racing fame were converted from standard Mini Coopers in the BMC Competitions Department. The author, who spent 22 years in 'Comps', reveals the secrets of specification, build technique and development of the famous Works Minis. The book includes contributions from Ginger Devlin (Cooper's chief mechanic) and 'Jumping Jeff' Williamson (Works Rallycross driver).

£16.99* • ISBN 978-1-904788-18-8

Brian Moylan spent 22 years with the Competition Department preparing cars for international rallies and travelling the world to provide service support. During this period, Big Healeys, Minis and TR7s were amongst the front-runners in the world rally scene, though many other BMC/BL models also saw use as rally cars. This is the fascinating tale as seen from a mechanic's point of view how BMC/BL rally cars evolved during this important period.

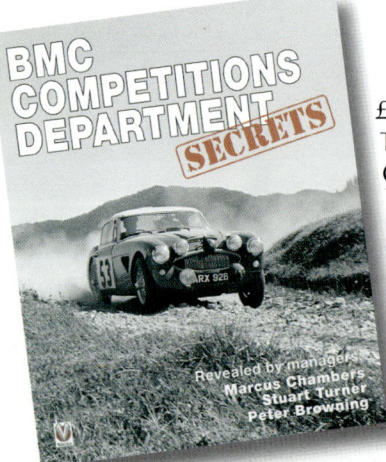

£24.99* • ISBN 978-1-904788-68-3

The inside story of the legendary BMC Works Competitions Department as told by the three competition managers. Based on previously unpublished internal memos and documents, and the recollections of the prime movers, here are the ups and downs, and the politics of big time competition in an exciting era.

£35.99* • ISBN 978-1-903706-97-8

This book covers the pre-WRC golden years, the Rally of the Forest period. With access to crew notes and manufacturers' archives, and containing many previously unpublished pictures, the history and excitement of the RAC International Rally of Great Britain has been captured in *RAC Rally Action!*

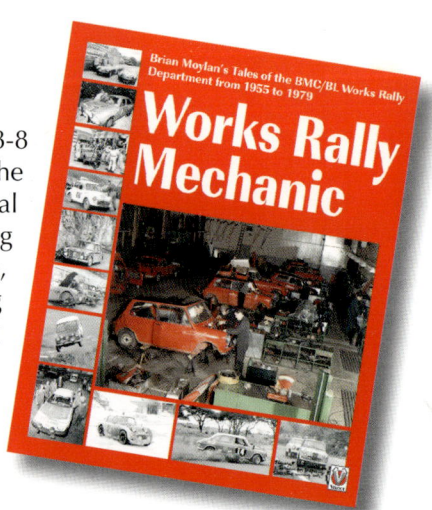

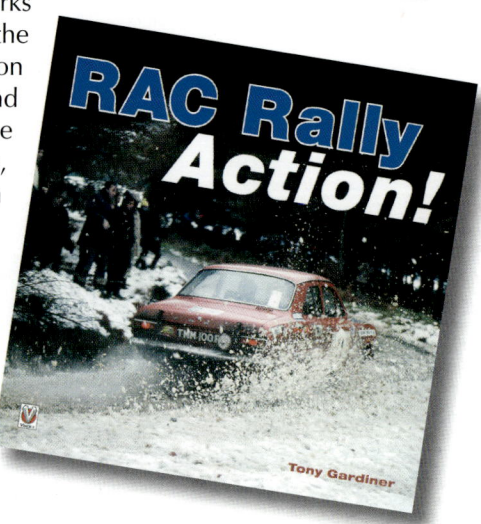

128

*p&p extra. Prices subject to change.